A Journey to Peace

Healing Through Love

Kimi Hadzima

Volume 1

A Journey to Peace: Healing Through Love, Volume 1
© 2025 Kimi Hadzima

Foreword by Reverend John F. Payne, Ph.D.

Published by **Kimi Hadzima**
Printed in the United States of America

First Edition

ISBN: 978-1-970250-00-8

This first volume is lovingly dedicated to:

Rev. Andy and Kim Oliver

Your love has left an impact that will
ripple through time.

The way you give of yourselves,
the way you care,
and the way you love
is a light that cannot be hidden.

May these pages carry forward even a fraction
of the influence your lives have had on mine!

TABLE OF CONTENTS

FOREWORD

Are you ready to move forward with your life? Do you want to let go of a past that hurts you or holds you back? *A Journey to Peace: Healing Through Love* will provide you with a guide to a new life sharing helpful new paths for living. You will become more self-assured as well as finding an inner peace and strength that you may not know existed.

Kimi has gone through the defeat, hell and abuse of life herself. But she found a way back to a whole life and a smile. Her book will help you find that place you are looking for.

The format of the book must be mentioned: Scripture, context, personal application, call to action and prayer. You will be guided from the written Word, through her revelations, and to a call to action for YOU. Then meaningful prayer will bring you to that new place you wish to be.

The Reverend John F. Payne, Ph.D.

INTRODUCTION

Welcome to Volume 1 of *A Journey to Peace: Healing Through Love*

This book is the story of my journey toward peace—one step at a time, one word at a time, one breath at a time. It's not a straight line, and it's far from perfect; however, it is reflective of my life, my struggles, and the ways I've found healing through love.

You'll find pieces of my story here: places where I was broken, times when I doubted myself, and moments when I began to believe I could be whole again. My reflections aren't meant to tell you how to live, but to open a window into how I've walked through my own pain, confusion, and growth.

Your journey may look very different from mine, exactly as it should be. My hope is that as you read, you'll find encouragement to keep going in your own way, at your own pace. If this book only helps one person find even a sliver of peace, it has fulfilled its purpose.

Each entry follows a rhythm: a focus, a reflection, a personal application, an invitation to act, and a Prayer. These are not rules; they're simply patterns that have helped me. Take what resonates. Leave what doesn't. Use these pages as a companion for your own healing, not a prescription for what it must look like.

CONTEXTUAL REFLECTION AND PERSONAL APPLICATION

Before we begin, I want to share how each section is designed to guide you. Every passage begins with the *Red Letters* and *Contextual Reflection*, where I look at the history, meaning, and heart behind the words spoken by Jesus. This isn't about theology or doctrine; it's about understanding the humanity, compassion, and purpose within His words.

Following that, you'll find a *Personal Application*—where those same truths meet real life. This is where I connect what I've learned to my own experiences, struggles, and growth. My hope is that as you read, you'll see yourself somewhere in these pages and feel invited to pause, reflect, and explore what healing looks like for you.

What Are the Red Letters?

You may notice that this book references the phrase *Red Letters*. In many Bibles, the words spoken by Jesus are printed in red, to set them apart from the rest of the text. These are the words recorded by those who walked closest with Him, passed down through centuries.

Whether you consider yourself religious or not, these words have carried power, hope, and comfort for generations. They speak to *identity, healing, love, and peace*. My reflections are built around them because they've shaped my journey. You don't need to be a Christian to find value here. Wherever you are in life, these truths can meet you there.

So welcome, friend. This is my journey, offered to you as a companion for yours. May you find peace, and may you find love written in these pages.

LET IT BE SO NOW

"Let it be so now; it is proper for us to do this to fulfill all righteousness." —Matthew 3:15

Contextual Reflection

These are the first recorded words of Jesus in Matthew; spoken not from a stage, but from the riverbank.

John the Baptist tried to stop Him: "I need to be baptized by You." But Jesus didn't hesitate. He didn't overexplain. He simply said, "Let it be so now."

He didn't need to be baptized, but He chose to be. He chose humility. He chose obedience. And He didn't need anyone's approval to do it.

He didn't need John to understand before stepping forward. He moved with God, not the crowd. That is the model. [2,3,4,6]

Personal Application

I think of how many times I've delayed obedience; waiting for someone to understand, agree, or validate my next step. That's codependency. Jesus confronts it with just five words: *"Let it be so now."*

Not later.
Not when it makes sense.
Not when it's safe.
Not after people approve.
JUST NOW.

Jesus shows me that faithfulness doesn't come with applause. Obedience doesn't need permission. And real freedom comes when I stop needing others to be okay with who I am or what I do.

This is how I want to walk into what God is building through me, through *LumaRise*.

Not explaining. Not shrinking. Not managing anyone's feelings.

Just saying yes.

And I've watched what happens when I do. When I choose intimacy with God over worrying what others think of me, something in me loosens. I can breathe deeper, and the anxiety begins to ease.

This is the quiet, Spirit-led freedom I never knew I could have.

Call to Action

Take a moment to ask:

- *Am I delaying obedience while waiting for approval?*
- *Is codependency hiding behind "humility"?*
- *What's one thing God has whispered that I haven't acted on?*

Take one quiet, unapproved step of obedience today. Let it be so now.

Prayer

Jesus,

Break the pattern in me that seeks validation before obedience. Help me walk in quiet trust, free from the weight of others' opinions. Please show me what it looks like to move in step with the Father—without apology, without delay. I want to follow You like that. Let it be so now.

Amen.

> *"It is written: 'Man shall not live on bread alone, but on every word that comes from the mouth of God.'"* —Matthew 4:4
>
> *"It is also written: 'Do not put the Lord your God to the test.'"* —Matthew 4:7
>
> *"Away from me, Satan! For it is written: 'Worship the Lord your God, and serve him only.'"* —Matthew 4:10

Contextual Reflection

Fresh from His baptism and the Father's voice declaring Him beloved, Jesus is led into the wilderness. After forty days of fasting, hungry and alone, the enemy shows up.

This moment isn't just about temptation; it's about identity. Each attack begins with, "If you are the Son of God…"—aimed at twisting what God already confirmed.

Jesus doesn't argue or explain. He simply responds with what is written. He shows us that temptation targets our identity, especially when we're weak or freshly affirmed. The way through is truth—clear, steady, and spoken with authority. [1,2,4,6]

Personal Application

For years, I let the enemy define me through echoes of abuse and lies. Even now, as I walk through healing, the whispers still come:

> *"If you were really healed…"*
> *"If you were really called…"*

But like Jesus, I don't have to prove my worth. Healing isn't the absence of temptation, it's knowing who I am when it comes. His Word anchors me.

If you grew up being told you were broken, too much, or never enough, hear this: you are not the lies spoken over you.

You are His.

In Christ, we can replace false identities with truth and rebuild our inner dialogue on His Word, not our wounds.

Call to Action

Take a moment to ask:

- *Where am I still trying to earn what God already declared over me?*

Write down three truths about who He says you are. Keep them where you'll see them daily (I write them on my bathroom mirror in dry erase markers). When doubt rises, answer with: "It is written…"

Prayer

Jesus,

Thank You for showing me how to face temptation without losing my identity. When the old voices return, remind me of what is written. Help me stop striving for approval and live as the beloved child You've already named me.

Amen.

POOR IN SPIRIT

"Blessed are the poor in spirit, for theirs is the kingdom of heaven." —Matthew 5:3

Contextual Reflection

When Jesus opened His Sermon on the Mount, He began with a blessing that flipped human thinking upside down. In His world, as in ours, people believed that wealth, status, and outward power were signs of God's favor. But Jesus said the opposite: poverty of spirit—the honest awareness of our need, our emptiness, our inability to save ourselves—was the very doorway into the kingdom of heaven.

To be "poor in spirit" is not about financial poverty, nor is it self-hatred. It is the humility of knowing we cannot stand before God on our own strength. It's the cry of the soul that admits, I need You, Lord. This is the starting point of faith, the foundation for healing and wholeness. [2,3,4,6]

Personal Application

For much of my life, I tried to fill my emptiness with anything but God—validation from others, control, striving for perfection. I thought if I could perform well enough, maybe the hollow ache inside would go away. But it never did.

Maybe someone would notice. Maybe someone would love me. Maybe, just maybe, the emptiness inside me would be filled with something…anything.

But all the attempts to fill the void while hiding all my secrets left me empty, the poorest I could be in spirit. And boy was I surprised to learn that is exactly where Jesus meets me, every single time. The moments when I felt most unworthy, most broken, most lost were the very moments when the kingdom of heaven cracked open before me. God didn't despise my poverty; He met me there.

This scripture became real to me, as I am the poor in spirit. When I admitted that my life was unmanageable without God, healing finally began. That simple act of surrender, acknowledging my powerlessness, was the start of freedom. It was in letting go of my illusion of control that I finally experienced His grace.

Call to Action

Take a moment to ask:

- *Where do I feel poor in spirit right now?*
- *Where am I empty, needy, or weak?*

Instead of covering it up, bring it honestly to God. Remember that this very place of lack is the place Jesus called 'blessed.'

Prayer

Lord,

Thank You for loving me in my poverty of spirit. Teach me to stop hiding my weakness and to see it as the doorway to Your kingdom. Fill the places I cannot fill on my own and remind me that my need is not a curse but a blessing.

Amen.

THOSE WHO MOURN

"Blessed are those who mourn, for they will be comforted."
—Matthew 5:4

Contextual Reflection

In a world that avoids pain at all costs, Jesus speaks something shocking: mourning is blessed. Grief isn't weakness, failure, or punishment—it's sacred ground where God's comfort shows up. In Jewish tradition, mourning was a communal act; no one grieved alone. When Jesus said those who mourn would be comforted, He was declaring that God Himself draws near and wraps His arms around the brokenhearted.

The blessing isn't in the loss itself, but in what the loss opens: a raw, vulnerable space where God can pour His presence into us. Jesus teaches us that we were never meant to mourn by ourselves. The Holy Spirit is God living in us, whispering comfort and reminding us that His presence never leaves, even when grief feels overwhelming. His dwelling place within us is always kept safe when we live in love with Him. [2,3,7]

Personal Application

For years, I ran from mourning. I stuffed my grief deep down, slapped on a smile, pretended I was fine. Crying felt dangerous, either someone would exploit my vulnerability, or the tears might never stop once they started. So, I hid it.

But ignoring grief doesn't erase it. It festers. It leaks out in countless ways. For me, it looked like people-pleasing, perfectionism, and addictions—always seeking yet never finding.

When I finally let myself mourn, something unexpected happened. Instead of drowning me, my tears washed me clean. In the very moments I thought sorrow would undo me, I found God's arms holding me.

This scripture became real in my healing. When I began to believe that God truly cared for me and had the power to restore me, I found the courage to grieve honestly. Mourning became less about falling apart and more about letting Him step in. Every time I allowed myself to mourn, His comfort was there waiting.

Call to Action

Take a moment to ask:

- *Where are you holding back tears?*
- *What grief have you been too afraid to face?*

Instead of pushing it down, invite God into it. Let yourself feel it, even if just for a moment. Your tears are not wasted—they are a signal to heaven, and Jesus has promised comfort.

Prayer

Lord,

Thank You for not shame me for my tears but call me blessed in them. Teach me to stop running from grief and instead to bring it to You. Hold me close in my mourning and let Your comfort be the healing I need.

Amen.

"Blessed are the meek, for they will inherit the earth."
—Matthew 5:5

Contextual Reflection

When Jesus spoke these words, He upended the values of His culture (and ours). The world celebrates strength, dominance, and self-assertion. But Jesus said it is the meek—the gentle, the humble, the surrendered—who will inherit the earth.

Meekness isn't weakness. In Scripture, meekness is choosing humility over pride, surrender over self-assertion, and trust in God's justice rather than taking matters into our own hands. Jesus Himself embodied meekness—powerful yet gentle, surrendered yet strong.

By promising the meek an inheritance, Jesus pointed to a kingdom truth: the ones who stop clawing to gain power and control end up receiving everything. [2,4,6]

Personal Application

Growing up, I thought that meekness was passivity. I believed turning the other cheek meant letting them hit me again, allowing others to hurt, take advantage of, or abuse me. I struggled with this idea and thought meekness meant staying silent.

But true meekness isn't about accepting mistreatment. It's about trusting God with justice while still setting healthy boundaries that protect the heart He gave me.

Surrender was one of the hardest lessons for me. I thought being strong meant keeping control, holding it all together, making sure no one saw my cracks—hiding all the things I thought were bad.

This exhausting way of living left me clinging to a control I never really had.

When I started loosening my grip—admitting my codependency and perfectionism and releasing the need to be the fixer or the perfectly put-together one—I discovered a strange kind of strength. The less I controlled and the more I stepped out of denial, the freer I became.

Meekness showed up in my healing as the courage to trust God's hands more than my own. I thought surrender meant losing everything, but it turned out to be the way I gained everything that mattered—peace, joy, and a future I never thought I'd see.

This scripture became real in my healing. When I committed my life and will to Christ's care instead of my own, I found rest. What felt like weakness turned out to be the very doorway into strength.

Call to Action

Take a moment to ask:

- *Where am I still clinging to control?*
- *Where do I need to surrender instead of striving?*

Write it down and release it in prayer, even if it feels scary. Remember, meekness doesn't shrink you, it sets you free.

Prayer

Jesus,

Teach me the beauty of meekness. Show me that surrender isn't weakness but the path to true strength. Help me to release control into Your hands and trust that You will give me more than I could ever take for myself.

Amen.

HUNGER AND THIRST FOR RIGHTEOUSNESS

"Blessed are those who hunger and thirst for righteousness, for they will be filled." —Matthew 5:6

Contextual Reflection

Hunger and thirst are primal desires, warning us that something essential is missing. Jesus used this imagery to describe the longing of the soul for righteousness: to be right with God, to see His justice, to live in alignment with His ways. The world often urges us to crave wealth, success, recognition, or comfort. But Jesus redirected our deepest appetites toward God Himself.

Righteousness here is not about self-righteousness or perfectionism, but about relationship—being rightly connected to God and living out His character. And the promise is profound: those who long for Him will be filled. Not with scraps or leftovers, but with the fullness of His presence and His peace. [2,4,6]

Personal Application

For much of my life, I tried to satisfy my inner hunger with things that could never truly fill me—relationships, achievements, distractions, and especially the approval of others. I thought if I could just get enough of those things, maybe the ache inside would go away. But the hunger always returned, emptier than before.

When I began to pursue God instead—His Word, His presence, His righteousness—I discovered a different kind of fullness. Circumstances didn't change overnight, but my heart did. Once I fell in love with Him and truly surrendered, something inside me shifted. The more I leaned into Him, the less desperate I felt to fill the void with temporary fixes.

This verse became a turning point in my healing. My soul's hunger wasn't a sign of weakness but an invitation to feast on the only One who could satisfy me. The thirst I once tried to quench with control, perfectionism, and codependency was finally met in the living water of Christ.

Call to Action

Take a moment to ask:

- *What am I craving most right now?*
- *Is it something temporary, or is it God's righteousness?*

Be honest about where your appetite is pulling you. Then, take one step today to turn that hunger toward Him—through prayer, scripture, or simply sitting in His presence.

Prayer

God,

I confess that I often chase after things that can never satisfy my soul. Redirect my hunger and thirst toward You. Fill me with Your righteousness and let me find my satisfaction in Your presence alone.

Amen.

"Blessed are the merciful, for they will be shown mercy."
—Matthew 5:7

Contextual Reflection

Mercy is compassion in action. It is not just feeling sorry for someone, but extending grace, forgiveness, and kindness—even when it costs us. In a culture that prizes revenge and keeping score, Jesus promises blessing for those who choose mercy instead.

Mercy reflects the very heart of God. He shows us compassion in our weakness, forgiveness in our failure, and patience in our stumbling. As we receive His mercy, we are called to extend it outward and inward—becoming vessels of His grace, both toward others and ourselves, allowing God's compassion to soften our shame and teaching us to walk gently with our own healing hearts.[4,6,7]

Personal Application

Because I could not have mercy for myself, I was incapable of having it for anyone else, though I was often quicker to forgive others' shortcomings than my own. In my healing, I discovered that mercy is a strength. Therapy taught me the concept of forgiveness, but my bitterness toward my abusers never truly settled until I stepped outside of myself and started walking with Jesus.

Extending mercy did not excuse abuse or tolerate mistreatment, it meant I could stop letting bitterness poison my heart and twist my thoughts. When I truly internalized that forgiveness was not about the person who hurt me, I found freedom.

And when I began to show myself mercy—releasing the shame I carried and letting God's grace wash over me—I could finally extend that same compassion outward. Mercy healed what judgment only deepened.

I no longer hang my head as I walk because my Father tells me, *"I forgive you, My child!"*

Call to Action

Take a moment to ask:

- *Who do I need to show mercy to today, including myself?*

Name one person and one introspection and pray for God's strength to extend grace in both.

Prayer

Lord,

Thank You for the mercy You've poured out on me. Teach me to be merciful as You are to me. Free me from bitterness and fill me with compassion.

Amen.

THE PURE IN HEART

"Blessed are the pure in heart, for they will see God."
—Matthew 5:8

Contextual Reflection

Purity of heart is not about perfection; it is about undivided devotion. To be pure in heart is to align our intentions, desires, and motives with God's, free from pretense or hidden agendas.

Jesus promised that the pure in heart would see God. Not only someday in heaven, but here and now seeing His hand at work, His presence in daily life, His face in unexpected places. [4,6]

Personal Application

For years, my heart was divided. I chased God with one hand while clinging to unhealthy habits, approval, and control with the other. I wanted His blessing without fully surrendering—even begging for my calling and purpose before I was ready. My vision of Him was blurred by the clutter I refused to release.

As healing deepened, I learned that purity of heart wasn't something I could achieve through striving. It came through surrender; layer by layer, letting Him clean out shame, fear, and self-protection. Each release drew me closer, until each step of surrender became strides toward fully loving Him.

And then in the sweetest ways, I began to see God. Not just in church or scripture, but in conversations, in nature, in moments of laughter and tears. Purity of heart opened my eyes to His presence everywhere—to every small gift, even the fresh scent of a flower that catches my gaze.

Call to Action

Take a moment to ask:

- *What is dividing my heart right now?*

Pray for God to clear away distractions so you can see Him more clearly.

Prayer

Lord,

I pray that you give me a pure heart; one that is fully Yours. Remove what clouds my vision and let me see You in everything.

Amen.

"Blessed are the peacemakers, for they will be called children of God." —Matthew 5:9

Contextual Reflection

Jesus didn't say "peacekeepers"—those who avoid conflict at all costs—but *peacemakers*. Making peace is active, intentional, and often costly. It requires stepping into brokenness with courage and love.

When we make peace, we reflect the heart of God, who reconciled us to Himself through Christ. That's why peacemakers are called children of God, they look like their Father. [4,6,7]

Personal Application

For much of my life, I was the scapegoat which deeply confused peacekeeping and peacemaking. I thought staying silent, avoiding conflict, or smoothing everything over was the way to peace—the way to stop the abuse. But all it did was bury pain and allow dysfunction to grow.

My healing taught me that true peace doesn't come from avoidance. It comes from addressing wounds, speaking truth in love, and reconciling where possible. Sometimes making peace meant setting boundaries, other times it meant extending forgiveness—it always meant letting God heal those parts of me because I couldn't.

When I chose peacemaking over people-pleasing, I stepped into my identity as God's child in a deeper way. I'm learning to allow God to fight those battles.

Call to Action

Take a moment to ask:

- *Where is God calling me to be a peacemaker today in my relationships, family, workplace, or my own heart?*

Take one step toward that peace.

Prayer

Lord,

Please make me a peacemaker. Give me courage to face conflict with love and wisdom. Use me to reflect Your heart of reconciliation.

Amen.

"Blessed are those who are persecuted because of righteousness, for theirs is the kingdom of heaven. Blessed are you when people insult you, persecute you and falsely say all kinds of evil against you because of me. Rejoice and be glad, because great is your reward in heaven, for in the same way they persecuted the prophets who were before you."
—Matthew 5:10-12

Contextual Reflection

Jesus prepared His followers for the cost of discipleship. Living for righteousness and truth will not always win applause; sometimes it brings rejection, insult, or even persecution. Yet He called this a blessing, not a curse, because it aligns us with Him.

The promise is clear: the kingdom of heaven belongs to those who endure for His sake. Our suffering becomes part of the greater story of redemption. [2,4]

Personal Application

I used to crave approval so deeply that the thought of rejection terrified me. I wanted everyone to like me, to think I was good enough. But living for other's approval left me constantly empty, anxious, and feeling unworthy. I sought my identity in what others told me it was.

As I grow in Christ, I'm learning who He says I am. Following Him sometimes means being misunderstood, judged, or even rejected. Sharing my testimony hasn't always been easy, as not everyone understands. But I've learned that the approval of God is worth far more than that of people.

This Beatitude reminds me that my healing and my story will not always be celebrated, but they will always be covered in His blessing. My reward isn't in people's acceptance, but in His eternal promise.

Call to Action

Take a moment to ask:

- *Where am I holding back out of fear of rejection or ridicule?*

Pray for courage to stand firm in righteousness, even when it costs you.

Prayer

Lord,

I ask that you give me strength to endure rejection and courage to stand in righteousness. Remind me that my reward is in You, not in the approval of others. Thank You that the kingdom of heaven is mine in Christ.

Amen.

SALT AND LIGHT

Contextual Reflection

Salt preserves and flavors; light guides and reveals. Both are essential, both are purposeful. Jesus didn't say, "Try to become salt and light." He said *you are*. Our identity in Him is not optional or hidden. The danger is when salt loses its distinctiveness, or when light is hidden away. Then the very purpose of our existence is muted. [2,4,6]

Personal Application

For years, I was that person who hid my spirituality. I believed but didn't walk in faith. My salt was bland, and my light was buried under shame and fear. I was afraid of judgment, afraid of being "too much," afraid that if people saw the real me, they would walk away. So, I kept silent, thinking it was safer.

But the truth was, I didn't yet trust Jesus. I wanted His comfort without surrender, His blessing without obedience.

Healing shifted that. As He began restoring me, I realized my story—my struggles, my scars, my survival—wasn't meant to stay hidden. Salt only preserves what it touches. Light only matters when it shines in the dark. When I finally trusted Him, I started to live out loud. Not to draw attention to me (I was already good at that), but to point to Him.

Now, when I share my story, when I speak His name, when I let my faith be seen, I feel that light inside me brighten—and my tears of joy flow uncontrollably. I realize that even small acts of obedience, like a word of kindness or a moment of honesty, can flavor someone else's life with hope.

Call to Action

Take a moment to ask:

- *Where am I tempted to hide my faith?*
- *How can I bring my faith out in the open, into the light?*

Bring that place to God and ask Him for the courage to shine; not for your glory, but for His.

Prayer

Lord,

You have called me salt and light. Forgive me for the times I've hidden out of fear. Teach me to live openly, to flavor the world with Your grace, and to shine with Your love. May everything I do point back to You.

Amen.

> *"Do not think that I have come to abolish the Law or the
> Prophets; I have not come to abolish them but to fulfill them...
> Unless your righteousness surpasses that of the Pharisees and
> the teachers of the law, you will certainly not enter the
> kingdom of heaven." —Matthew 5:17-20*

Contextual Reflection

Jesus' words startled His listeners. Many expected Him to replace
the Law, but He revealed that He came to fulfill it—to bring it to
completion. The Law revealed God's holiness but couldn't
transform hearts. It could guide and convict, but only Jesus heals
and renews from within.

The Pharisees were meticulous about rules yet missed God's heart.
Jesus raised the standard, pointing to inner righteousness—
authentic surrender that only comes through Him, not through
outward performance.[2,3,4]

Personal Application

For much of my life, I lived like a Pharisee in disguise. I wanted to
look "good" on the outside, perfectly put together and never
showing my cracks. I thought righteousness was about appearances:
doing all the right things so people would believe I had it together.
But inside, I was carrying shame, fear, and unhealed anger toward
my abusers.

God had many walls to tear down within me—shame, fear, self-
protection—and this connects directly to Jesus' teaching:
outwardly, I may have looked fine, but inwardly He was preparing
me for transformation.

This wasn't me doing anything in my own strength, it was God.
And He used even my hidden struggles to show me that the Law
was never meant to be a checklist I could conquer. It wasn't

performance but a mirror, revealing my heart and my need for Him. My perception of righteousness could never measure up, and that was the point. Only His grace could.

That grace became tangible when I entered Celebrate Recovery for the first time. I realized this was the place! God brought me here to stop hiding and allow Him to tear down all of the walls and help me step into each room with Him. In that safe space, I learned to stop hiding behind appearances and start walking in honesty. Celebrate Recovery gave me tools, but more than that, it gave me a place where Jesus could meet me in my brokenness. That's where surrender became real and where I began to experience freedom.

As I surrendered, I found freedom in honesty. My healing didn't come from hiding flaws but from bringing them into His light. True righteousness wasn't about pretending, it was about letting Him write His law on my heart.

Call to Action

Take a moment to ask:

- *Am I relying on outward appearances of faith, or am I letting Jesus transform me inwardly?*

Release the need to prove yourself and invite Him to shape your heart.

Prayer

Lord,

Thank You for fulfilling what I could never carry out. Forgive me for the times I've tried to measure up by appearances. Thank You for using Celebrate Recovery and other tools to draw me closer to Your truth. Write Your law on my heart and let my life reflect authentic love, not empty performance.

Amen.

Anger and Reconciliation

> *"You have heard that it was said to the people long ago, 'You shall not murder, and anyone who murders will be subject to judgment.' But I tell you that anyone who is angry with a brother or sister will be subject to judgment... Therefore, if you are offering your gift at the altar and there remember that your brother or sister has something against you, leave your gift there in front of the altar. First go and be reconciled to them; then come and offer your gift."* —Matthew 5:21-26

Contextual Reflection

Jesus goes beyond the commandment against murder to expose the deeper issue of the heart: anger, resentment, and broken relationships. Murder begins with bitterness, and Jesus shows that even harboring anger puts us under judgment. His teaching calls us to reconciliation, valuing restored relationships over ritual or outward acts of worship. God cares about the posture of our hearts toward others as much as the sacrifices we bring to Him. [2,4]

Personal Application

For years, I carried anger toward my abusers. I didn't want to call it bitterness, but deep down I knew the pain was shaping how I saw myself and how I related to others. Yet God never allowed that anger to completely rule my life. Even when I wrestled with the weight of injustice, He preserved my heart from being hardened beyond repair. That was His grace at work, keeping me in a place where His love could still reach me.

Over time, I learned that forgiveness didn't mean excusing their behavior, it meant releasing the grip their actions had on my soul. Letting go of anger opened the door to grace. It allowed me to separate who they were from what they did, and to entrust justice into God's hands. When I came to that place, I found myself no longer bound by the chains that had wrapped around my heart, mind, and soul.

Celebrate Recovery gave me a safe space to walk this out. Through honest conversations, making amends, and choosing forgiveness again and again, I began to taste freedom. I realized reconciliation isn't just about repairing relationships with others—it's about being reconciled to peace within myself and with God. He guides me to live it out daily, addressing issues as they arise so I don't carry the guilt of waiting or risk never addressing them at all. That's where healing took root, and where His grace became more than words— it became my reality.

Call to Action

Take a moment to ask:

- *Am I holding onto anger that keeps me chained to the past?*

Pray for the courage to release it to God and let His grace bring freedom.

Prayer

Lord,

Thank You for preserving my heart even when anger tried to consume me. Teach me to release my pain into Your hands and to forgive as You forgive me. Free me from the chains of resentment and let Your peace rule in my heart.

Amen.

LUST AND THE HEART

> *"You have heard that it was said, 'You shall not commit adultery.' But I tell you that anyone who looks at a woman lustfully has already committed adultery with her in his heart. If your right eye causes you to stumble, gouge it out and throw it away. It is better for you to lose one part of your body than for your whole body to be thrown into hell. And if your right hand causes you to stumble, cut it off and throw it away. It is better for you to lose one part of your body than for your whole body to go into hell."* —Matthew 5:27-30

Contextual Reflection

Jesus exposes how sin begins long before outward actions. Adultery isn't just a physical act; it starts in the heart and mind. His teaching cuts to the root of desire, showing that holiness isn't about managing appearances but about cultivating purity within. The hyperbolic language of "gouging out an eye" or "cutting off a hand" illustrates the seriousness of removing anything that leads us toward sin. He calls us to radical honesty and decisive action in dealing with temptation. [2,4]

Personal Application

For me, this scripture isn't about lust in the narrow sense alone, it's about misplaced desires and unhealthy attachments of the heart. For years, I longed for things that would numb my pain rather than heal it: alcohol, marijuana, intimate relationships, approval, and attention. My desperate need for validation led me to codependent patterns that looked like comfort but only deepened my brokenness. While these weren't always visible to others, they revealed the wounds inside me that I struggled to surrender.

God has been teaching me to deal honestly with these desires, not to pretend they aren't there. In Celebrate Recovery, I continue to learn to name my struggles and bring them into the light instead of hiding them. The process isn't about shame but about surrender; it's about cutting off what is destructive before it consumes more of me. Jesus shows me again and again that true freedom isn't found in suppressing desire but in redirecting it toward Him, the only One who can truly fulfill.

I am not "healed," I am healing. With each issue I surrender, He transforms my heart and soul little by little. Some chains have been broken, but others I still wrestle with daily. As long as I remain in this life, the process will continue. Yet I have found that with every surrender, I taste more freedom, more strength to walk away from destructive patterns, and more clarity to choose healthier paths. The more I release, the freer I become.

Call to Action

Take a moment to ask:

- *What desires am I clinging to that keep me from experiencing healing and freedom in Christ?*

Consider what radical steps you may need to take to cut off unhealthy patterns and invite God to purify your heart.

Prayer

Jesus,

I pray that you search my heart and reveal the desires that lead me away from You. Give me the courage to let go of what harms me and the strength to walk in purity and freedom. Teach me to find my fulfillment in You alone.

Amen.

DIVORCE AND FAITHFULNESS

"It has been said, 'Anyone who divorces his wife must give her a certificate of divorce.' But I tell you that anyone who divorces his wife, except for sexual immorality, makes her the victim of adultery, and anyone who marries a divorced woman commits adultery." —Matthew 5:31-32

Contextual Reflection

In Jesus' day, divorce had become casual and often self-serving. Men could dismiss their wives with little thought, leaving women vulnerable and dishonored. Jesus confronts this cultural norm, revealing God's deeper intent: marriage is meant to reflect covenant faithfulness, not convenience. His teaching reminds us that righteousness is not about finding loopholes but honoring God's design of committed love. While this passage is often misunderstood as rigid law, its heart is about protecting the vulnerable and upholding the sacredness of relationship. [2,4]

Personal Application

The first time I read this scripture, I was already divorced. I spent many moments with Jesus while wrestling with these words, because I had so much guilt and shame tied to the "divorced" label. I feared that it meant I was marked forever as unworthy.

But as I sat with Him on this today, I began to hear something different. Instead of condemnation, I heard Jesus calling me into healing. My story is not about failure; it is about His faithfulness in the middle of my brokenness.

Codependency, relationship addiction, alcohol, marijuana, and my desperate need for approval led me into unhealthy relationships where I settled for less than God's design. Divorce was one of the outcomes of that cycle. And yet, even there, God's grace met me.

After an entire adult life of relationship addiction, I finally surrendered it to God. For over a year now, I have not even had the desire to seek a romantic relationship. That freedom has been a gift of His healing—teaching me to rest first in Him rather than rushing to fill the void with another person.

What Jesus shows me here is that faithfulness isn't only about marriage vows; it's about learning to love as He loves—with consistency, honesty, and grace. In my journey, I've been learning to move from disposable patterns of connection toward covenant faithfulness, first with God and now with others.

Through healing, I've learned to stop running when things got uncomfortable. I've learned to commit, to show up, and to let others show up for me. God has been teaching me that the truest relationship, the one I can always depend on, is with Him. As I lean into that, my ability to form healthy, lasting relationships with others has begun to grow.

Call to Action

Take a moment to ask:

- *Where have I treated relationships as disposable instead of sacred?*
- *How might God be calling me to move from convenience toward covenant, with Him and with others?*

Prayer

Lord,

Please heal the broken places in me that still carry the weight of failed relationships. Thank You for meeting me in grace rather than condemnation. Teach me faithfulness and show me how to reflect Your covenant love in every relationship I enter.

Amen.

> *"You have heard that it was said, 'Eye for eye, and tooth for tooth.' But I tell you, do not resist an evil person. If anyone slaps you on the right cheek, turn to them the other cheek also. And if anyone wants to sue you and take your shirt, hand over your coat as well. If anyone forces you to go one mile, go with them two miles. Give to the one who asks you, and do not turn away from the one who wants to borrow from you."*
> —Matthew 5:38-42

Contextual Reflection

In the Old Testament, the principle of "eye for eye" was meant as a boundary for justice, limiting retaliation so it would not spiral into endless cycles of revenge. But by Jesus' day, people often used it to justify payback and holding grudges. Jesus raises the standard beyond mere fairness to radical grace. Instead of perpetuating cycles of harm, He calls His followers to absorb the offense, extend mercy, and trust God with justice. This isn't weakness but strength: choosing love over retaliation. [2,3,4,6]

Personal Application

There was a season when I dreamed of ways to retaliate against my abusers. I would replay scenes in my head, fantasizing about how I could make them pay. My anger became an endless loop that consumed my thoughts. When people told me, *"You have to love and respect your mother,"* I pushed back hard. *"She never respected or loved me. She didn't protect me. She allowed things to happen and inflicted so much herself. How could I ever love and respect that?"* I would insist, *"You don't understand—and no, I do not have to!"* For me, this teaching directly confronted my fantasies of revenge, exposing that my anger could never free me. It was only in grace that healing and peace could take root.

This wound was deep. It shaped much of my life, leaving scars I thought would never heal. But over time, God met me in that place. He didn't excuse what happened, but He began softening my heart. Slowly, He helped me see that forgiveness wasn't about denying the pain or pretending it was okay—it was about releasing my need for vengeance. Jesus' words pressed into my heart, pulling me out of fantasies of retaliation and guiding me into the freedom of grace.

I have come to forgive my mother, understanding that she did the best she knew how, even with all the ways she fell short. This forgiveness does not erase the scar—nor does it pardon the perpetrator—but it has brought me peace. I honor myself for surviving, and I honor God for giving me the grace to move from anger to release. By letting go of retaliation, I am no longer chained to bitterness. I live freer, lighter, and more open to His love.

Call to Action

Take a moment to ask:

- *Where am I still fantasizing about retaliation? Where does bitterness hold me hostage?*
- *How might God be inviting me to release the need for vengeance and instead choose His peace?*

Prayer

Lord,

You see the wounds and the scars that shaped me. You know the anger I carried and the fantasies of revenge I once held onto. Thank You for walking with me through that pain and teaching me that forgiveness is freedom. Help me continue to release vengeance and to trust You fully with justice. Fill my heart with Your peace so I may live unchained.

Amen.

"You have heard that it was said, 'Love your neighbor and hate your enemy.' But I tell you, love your enemies and pray for those who persecute you, that you may be children of your Father in heaven. He causes his sun to rise on the evil and the good, and sends rain on the righteous and the unrighteous. If you love those who love you, what reward will you get? Are not even the tax collectors doing that? And if you greet only your own people, what are you doing more than others? Do not even pagans do that? Be perfect, therefore, as your heavenly Father is perfect." —Matthew 5:43-48

Contextual Reflection

The call to love enemies may be the most radical teaching in the Sermon on the Mount. In a culture where hatred of enemies was accepted, Jesus turned everything upside down. He revealed the heart of the Father—a love that extends to both the righteous and the unrighteous, to both friend and foe. Loving those who love us is natural; but loving those who wound us, pray against us, or betray us requires divine strength. This is not about excusing sin or enabling abuse, it is about reflecting God's unrelenting grace. His love flows to all, and He invites us to take part in that radical, world-changing love. [2,3,4,6]

Personal Application

For years, I held deep anger toward people who hurt me. As a child, my older brother was cruel, setting me up for punishments and mocking me as I suffered. Later, as an adult, when we reunited after years apart, his words placed blame on me for escaping an abusive home—as if there were a "right" way for a 14-year-old to flee such horror. That moment broke my heart. I carried anger, resentment, and shame for many years, replaying the pain and punishing myself over and over.

This scripture has challenged me to pray for him, the very brother who hurt me and never understood my suffering. I have also learned about his own hidden pain and struggles that I never saw. None of which excuses his actions, but it has helped me understand that God loves him just as much as He loves me. Choosing to forgive and pray for him does not erase the scars, but it releases me from the weight of carrying resentment. It is not about declaring him innocent, it is about freeing my own heart so that God's love can flow more freely through me.

After an entire adult life of holding onto anger and resentment toward him, I finally gave this to God. This has been His healing in me, a transformation I never thought possible. Where pain and anger once stood, I have come to a place of forgiveness and love.

Call to Action

Take a moment to ask:

- *Who do I still hold anger against?*
- *Where might God be inviting me to pray for the very ones I feel don't deserve it?*
- *What would it look like to let His love flow through me, even toward those who have hurt me?*

Prayer

Lord,

Loving my enemies feels impossible without You. You know the pain I carry, the betrayals, and the deep scars left behind. Yet You call me to love and to pray, not out of my strength but Yours. Teach me to release resentment into Your hands, to forgive as You forgive, and to trust that You are the righteous Judge. Fill my heart with Your perfect love so that I may live in freedom and reflect Your grace.

Amen.

GIVING IN SECRET

"Be careful not to practice your righteousness in front of others to be seen by them. If you do, you will have no reward from your Father in heaven.

So when you give to the needy, do not announce it with trumpets, as the hypocrites do in the synagogues and on the streets, to be honored by others. Truly I tell you, they have received their reward in full.

But when you give to the needy, do not let your left hand know what your right hand is doing, so that your giving may be in secret. Then your Father, who sees what is done in secret, will reward you." —Matthew 6:1-4

Contextual Reflection

Jesus begins with giving. In His culture, generosity was often performed in public, a way of proving piety and status. But He turns that upside down: true righteousness doesn't need a stage. God sees what's hidden, and He delights in acts of compassion done quietly, for His eyes alone. [2,4,6]

Personal Application

I've struggled with self-worth my entire life, often tying my value to what I could do for others, sacrificing much for very little in return. Performing for love, approval, and acceptance became a way of life, rooted in what I lacked as a child. Before I fully allowed Jesus into my heart, I carried extremely low self-esteem, even though I still believed God could change everything. Over time, I fell away and stopped believing, but when I returned to Him, the journey of change began. It wasn't instantaneous, it unfolded slowly, layer by layer, as God showed me the truth about who I really am in Him.

Jesus has been teaching me that my worth is not found in people pleasing, high achievement, or always giving more than I have. Those patterns left me drained and empty, promising peace they could never deliver. Storing up treasures in heaven means checking where my heart leans—choosing to measure my worth not by possessions, performance, or approval, but by who I belong to. When I place my worth in Christ, I discover a treasure no one can take away.

Call to Action

Look for an opportunity to give quietly this week. It doesn't have to be big, maybe meeting a need, offering encouragement, or sharing resources. Do it in a way that no one else sees and let it be an offering between you and God alone.

Prayer

Father,

Teach me to give with a pure heart. Strip away any desire for recognition and let my generosity reflect Your love. Thank You for seeing what no one else sees.

Amen.

"And when you pray, do not be like the hypocrites, for they love to pray standing in the synagogues and on the street corners to be seen by others. Truly I tell you, they have received their reward in full.

But when you pray, go into your room, close the door and pray to your Father, who is unseen. Then your Father, who sees what is done in secret, will reward you.

And when you pray, do not keep on babbling like pagans, for they think they will be heard because of their many words. Do not be like them, for your Father knows what you need before you ask him.

This, then, is how you should pray: Our Father in heaven, hallowed be your name, your kingdom come, your will be done, on earth as it is in heaven. Give us today our daily bread. And forgive us our debts, as we also have forgiven our debtors. And lead us not into temptation, but deliver us from the evil one.

For if you forgive other people when they sin against you, your heavenly Father will also forgive you. But if you do not forgive others their sins, your Father will not forgive your sins."
—Matthew 6:5-15

Contextual Reflection

Prayer, at its core, is about intimacy with God, not performance. Jesus contrasts public display with private devotion, teaching that the Father rewards sincerity. The Lord's Prayer is both a pattern and a posture: honoring God, seeking His will, trusting Him for provision, confessing and forgiving, and asking for guidance. It distills the heart of discipleship into just a few lines. Forgiveness stands out—Jesus makes it clear that receiving it and extending it are inseparable. [1,2,4,6]

Personal Application

On my walks, when I know someone is nearby, I pause my prayer. I wait until I'm out of earshot before I continue. It's interesting that this became a natural rhythm, as though God has always put it on my heart that these are our moments together, not performances for others.

I also struggle with Jesus' words about babbling. At first, I felt it necessary to verbalize His responses, almost to prove to myself that I heard Him. I still do that at times, but I'm slowly learning to quiet my own words and let His truth settle deep in my soul before I move forward.

And then there's the Lord's Prayer. I return to it again and again. These words remind me to begin with God's glory, not my own agenda. They humble me to ask for only what I need for today, not that of tomorrow—reminding me that I am to take one thing at a time in healing. God's grace forgives and convicts me to forgive as well. He assures me His protection and deliverance are always right here and everywhere.

Call to Action

This week, commit to a time of secret prayer. Close the door, silence the distractions, and talk honestly with God. Pray the Lord's Prayer slowly, pausing after each phrase, and let the Spirit show you how each line speaks into your life today. Release someone you've struggled to forgive into His hands and ask Him to shape your heart through the act of forgiveness.

Prayer

Our Father in heaven,

Hallowed be Your name. May Your kingdom come, and Your will be done in me. Provide what I need today, forgive my sins, and help me forgive others. Lead me away from temptation and deliver me from evil. For Yours is the kingdom and the power and the glory forever.

Amen.

> *"When you fast, do not look somber as the hypocrites do, for they disfigure their faces to show others they are fasting. Truly I tell you, they have received their reward in full.*
>
> *But when you fast, put oil on your head and wash your face, so that it will not be obvious to others that you are fasting, but only to your Father, who is unseen; and your Father, who sees what is done in secret, will reward you." —Matthew 6:16-18*

Contextual Reflection

Fasting was common in Jewish life but often misused for display. Jesus calls His followers to fast in a way that is unseen—out of hunger for God, not human approval. True fasting is about humility and focus, not pity or prestige. [2,4]

Personal Application

When I've set aside distractions or comforts to focus on God, I've found new clarity and strength. It wasn't about proving my devotion to anyone else; it was about carving out space for Him to move in my life. For me, fasting has also meant giving up unhealthy attachments—like relationship addiction and codependency.

In Celebrate Recovery, I've been celebrating my clean time from intimate relationships, not to advertise it to the world or to look good, but to let God cleanse my heart and soul in this area. I'm not running around announcing that I'm single; rather, I'm surrendering this season to Him, trusting He will heal me and prepare me for healthy love when the time is right.

Lately, God has been showing me that even the label "single" can become a kind of mask—a way of defining myself by what I *don't* have instead of who I *belong to*. This season isn't about being single; it's about being *set apart*. I choose to be "off the market" out of obedience. I know this time is meant to be spent with Him.

I'm learning that fasting isn't just about food or relationships—it's about focus. It's about intimacy with the One who already sees me, knows me, and loves me completely.

Call to Action

Ask God to show you an issue, hurt, or habit that you need to surrender to Him. Maybe it's anger, control, codependency, fear, or something else that has taken root in your life. Commit to fasting from that pattern, laying it in His hands. Each time you feel the pull of it, turn your attention to God and invite Him to cleanse and heal you in that place.

Prayer

Father,

I hunger for more of You. Teach me to fast with humility, to seek You above all else, and to find strength in Your presence. As I surrender my hurts, habits, and hang-ups, cleanse me and make me whole. May every unseen sacrifice draw me closer to You.

Amen.

TREASURES IN HEAVEN

"Do not store up for yourselves treasures on earth, where moths and vermin destroy, and where thieves break in and steal. But store up for yourselves treasures in heaven, where moths and vermin do not destroy, and where thieves do not break in and steal. For where your treasure is, there your heart will be also." —Matthew 6:19-21

Contextual Reflection

Jesus redirects our attention from what is temporary to what is eternal. Earthly possessions and accomplishments can decay, be stolen, or disappear. Heavenly treasures—acts of love, service, forgiveness, and obedience—endure forever. Where we invest our time, attention, and resources reveal the true direction of our hearts.

This also speaks to how we often tie our self-worth to performance: people pleasing, high achievement, or always giving more than we have. Those may look like treasure in the moment, but they are fragile and exhausting. Jesus reminds us that our worth is not measured by performance or possessions, but by the eternal value we already have in Him. [2,4,6]

Personal Application

I've struggled with self-worth my entire life, always tying my value to what I could do for others, sacrificing much for very little in return. Performing for love, approval, and acceptance became a way of life, rooted in what I lacked as a child. Before I fully allowed Jesus into my heart, I carried extremely low self-esteem, even though I still believed God had a purpose for me. Over time, I fell away and stopped believing, but when I returned to Him, the journey of change began. It wasn't instantaneous—it unfolded over a 14-year revealing period, as He gradually showed me His truth.

By the time I was 50, I could finally see the depth of His work, instilling His truth into my soul on a level beyond words.

Jesus has been teaching me that my worth is not found in people pleasing, high achievement, or always giving more than I have. Those patterns left me drained and empty, promising peace they could never deliver. Storing up treasures in heaven means checking where my heart leans; choosing to measure my worth not by possessions, performance, or approval, but by who I belong to. When I place my worth in Christ, I discover a treasure no one can take away.

Call to Action

Take time this week to find one way you can shift your focus from performance or possessions toward heavenly treasure. Maybe it's releasing the need to please others, forgiving someone, or serving quietly without recognition. Let your actions point your heart toward eternity.

Prayer

Father,

Please help me treasure what lasts. Free me from chasing worth in things that fade. Redirect my heart to find its value in You alone, so my life reflects Your glory.

Amen.

THE EYE AS THE LAMP

"The eye is the lamp of the body. If your eyes are healthy, your whole body will be full of light. But if your eyes are unhealthy, your whole body will be full of darkness. If then the light within you is darkness, how great is that darkness!"
—Matthew 6:22-23

Contextual Reflection

The eye stands for our focus, the lens through which we interpret the world. A healthy eye fixed on God fills our whole life with light. But when our focus is clouded by greed, envy, fear, or distraction, even what seems like light may actually be darkness. [2,4,6]

Personal Application

As I've healed, I've realized how much my vision has changed. When I held on to pain and anger, I could only see life through that lens. Everything felt filtered through resentment and wounds. But as I began to dig into my past hurts and face the traumas that shaped me, I noticed my lens started to shift.

For me, that lens has slowly turned into compassion. I began to understand that those who hurt me were deeply hurting themselves. Their lives were marked by trauma, unhealed pain, and constant anger—they could only see the world through the red haze of their own suffering. Healing allowed me to step back and see differently, one hurt at a time, one issue at a time, one day at a time.

This shift began in therapy, when I reflected on the horrific things my parents and their siblings endured. Abuse was hidden, never corrected, and never punished. And as I've learned, what stays hidden always continues to wound. Recognizing their pain gave me clarity: my eyes no longer had to see through anger but could begin to see through God's light of compassion and truth.

Call to Action

Take a moment to ask:

- *Through what lens am I seeing the world right now? Is it pain, anger, fear, or compassion?*

Invite God to heal the hurts that cloud your vision and allow Him to slowly shift your perspective one issue at a time. As He clears your lens, let His light fill your life and shine through you.

Prayer

Lord,

My prayer today is that you make my eyes clear and fixed on You. Guard me from viewing life through fear or anger. Heal the hidden wounds that distort my vision. Fill me with Your light so it shines through every part of my life.

Amen.

SERVING TWO MASTERS

"No one can serve two masters. Either you will hate the one and love the other, or you will be devoted to the one and despise the other. You cannot serve both God and money."
—Matthew 6:24

Contextual Reflection

Jesus makes a bold and unambiguous statement: we cannot divide our loyalty. Money is not evil in itself, but it can become a master that competes with God for our devotion. And money is not the only rival—approval, control, relationships, fear, or even our own struggles can take the role of master in our lives. We are created for wholehearted service, not split allegiance, and anything that chains our hearts away from God will eventually leave us empty.[2,4,6]

Personal Application

For me, I struggled to focus on God because my struggles were always in the forefront of my mind, ruling every step I made.

How do I keep from being abandoned?

How do I keep from having to be alone?

How do I make sure that I do everything for everyone so that they will love me?

In the past, these were the questions that ruled my life. They were the things I couldn't live without, and they muddied any relationship I could have with Jesus. They felt more important because I believed I had to control them to keep myself safe.

Each struggle became a master of its own; a chain that bound me to fear, distraction, and self-reliance. These false masters pulled me away from the life God had planned. Real freedom began when I recognized those chains for what they were and began surrendering them to God's care one at a time, allowing Him to lead me instead.

Call to Action

Reflect honestly on what competes with God for your devotion. It might be money, but it could also be approval, relationships, fear, control, or even your own struggles. Name those false masters before Him, confess them, and begin surrendering them one by one. Choose this week to serve God above all, letting Him be the only Master of your life.

Prayer

Father,

I choose You as my only Master. Free me from the pull of divided loyalty. Teach me to trust You completely and let my devotion belong to You alone.

Amen.

"Do not judge, or you too will be judged. For in the same way you judge others, you will be judged, and with the measure you use, it will be measured to you.

Why do you look at the speck of sawdust in your brother's eye and pay no attention to the plank in your own eye? How can you say to your brother, 'Let me take the speck out of your eye,' when all the time there is a plank in your own eye? You hypocrite, first take the plank out of your own eye, and then you will see clearly to remove the speck from your brother's eye." —Matthew 7:1-5

Contextual Reflection

Jesus begins this section with a direct command not to judge others. But He's not banning discernment—He's warning against hypocritical, harsh judgment rooted in pride. The imagery of a person trying to remove a speck from someone else's eye while a plank juts from their own is intentionally ridiculous—He wants us to laugh at the absurdity. This isn't just moral teaching; it's a heart check.

This passage flows directly from Matthew 6's theme of inner versus outer righteousness. Jesus is after transformation from the inside out, not just polished appearances. In the Kingdom of God, we confront sin through the lens of humility and self-awareness, not superiority. He's teaching us to see clearly, but that only happens after we let Him clean our own vision. [2,4,6]

Personal Application

For many years, I struggled with religion because I felt judged by people in the church. As a child from a poor and majorly dysfunctional home, I was just trying to survive—but instead of love, I often received looks of shame or pity. That feeling of rejection built a wall in my heart, and I kept my distance from anything labeled "Christian" for 20 years.

It wasn't until Celebrate Recovery that I began to understand that hurt people hurt people, and the church is not for the perfect—it's for the broken. And I realized that I was just as judgmental as those who had once judged me. In my healing, I've come to see that church is exactly where all of God's children belong.

This scripture helped me recognize the plank in my own eye and now, Jesus and I are working on chipping away at it, speck by speck.

One of the hardest lessons in recovery has been realizing how my own unhealed places caused pain in others. I can't love well if I'm blind to my own brokenness. I can't hold others accountable without admitting my own faults first. That's the beauty of what Jesus is saying. He's not telling me to stop helping others. He's saying, *Let me help you first. Then you'll be safe to help them, too.*

Call to Action

If you've been wounded by judgment or find yourself quick to point fingers, ask Jesus to show you what's still hiding in your own heart. Invite Him to begin that healing work within you first. When we let Him restore our sight, we can finally see others the way He does—with truth and tenderness.

Prayer

Jesus,

Remove my blind spots. I don't want to be a hypocrite. Help me see myself clearly so I can walk in humility and extend grace. Teach me to lead with love, not judgment.

Amen.

SACRED THINGS IN SAFE SPACES

"Do not give dogs what is sacred; do not throw your pearls to pigs..." —Matthew 7:6

Contextual Reflection

In this verse, Jesus is not calling people pigs or dogs, He's using metaphor to teach discernment. Sacred things—truth, testimony, healing—aren't meant to be offered recklessly in spaces that will mock or trample them.

This follows the judgment passage for a reason. Once your vision is clear, you'll know when it's time to speak truth and when it's time to hold silence. In His wisdom, Jesus shows us that even in love, boundaries are holy. [2,3,4]

Personal Application

When I was in my late teens and early twenties, I told my story to anyone who would listen. I didn't understand what boundaries were. There were none in our home growing up, and the only form of discipline I knew was extreme and abusive. I had been told at ten years old that talking about your problems helped with the shame, so I thought sharing was healing.

But my story wasn't easy to hear. It wasn't sugar-coated or sanitized, it was disturbing. Over time, I stopped telling it altogether. The responses I got were either disbelief or cold indifference, and I started to believe my story didn't matter. Jesus had to show me that it *does* matter, in the right spaces. I was in my late 40s when I finally started sharing again with others outside of therapy, when I found Celebrate Recovery.

Now, I know that protecting my healing doesn't mean hiding it; it means honoring it. My story is a pearl, and pearls belong in trusted hands. Discernment isn't about silence; it's about love—love for my journey, and love for those who are truly ready to hold it with care.

Call to Action

Take a moment to ask:

- *Is there someone in my life who keeps disregarding my sacred things or spaces?*
- *What boundaries can I set up to ensure my sacred things or spaces are protected?*

You're allowed to set boundaries. Ask Jesus for clarity and courage. Healing sometimes begins with a holy, "No."

Prayer

Lord,

Give me wisdom to know where to pour out and where to hold back. Show me who is ready for truth and who needs prayer from afar. Keep my sacred things safe in You.

Amen.

THE FATHER WHO GIVES GOOD GIFTS

"Ask and it will be given to you; seek and you will find; knock and the door will be opened to you. For everyone who asks receives; the one who seeks finds; and to the one who knocks, the door will be opened.

Which of you, if your son asks for bread, will give him a stone? Or if he asks for a fish, will give him a snake? If you, then, though you are evil, know how to give good gifts to your children, how much more will your Father in heaven give good gifts to those who ask him!" —Matthew 7:7-11

Contextual Reflection

Jesus isn't offering a magic formula here; He's revealing the heart of the Father. These verses invite us into persistence, not performance. We're told to ask, seek, and knock not just once, but continuously. And what fuels that persistence is trust: trust that the One we're calling on is good, generous, and deeply personal.

He uses a relatable example, parents giving good gifts to their children, to drive the point home. If flawed, earthly people can still care for their children, how much more will our perfect Father respond with love? He isn't distant or stingy. He's waiting, ready to pour out what we truly need. [2,4,6]

Personal Application

I felt like I had to act the act with no idea how to walk the walk. I spent years trying to earn God's attention, afraid to be too needy or ask the wrong way. I believed in Him, but I didn't really trust Him. I didn't know Him at all.

Looking back, I realize I never fully did all three. I would ask, but I didn't seek. I didn't knock. When nothing happened, I thought it was because I'd failed somehow. But the truth is, I hadn't yet surrendered. I didn't believe He would come through *for me.*

When I finally fell in love with Him and trust replaced fear, I started doing all three. I laid my burdens down, I began to seek His heart, and I knocked with faith. That's when I discovered the truth about God: He wasn't holding out on me—He was waiting for my trust to open the door. *I was the one holding out on Him.*

Now, when I come to Him, I come like a daughter tugging on His clothes asking, "Daddy, what do I do?"—not as an employee or a beggar—as His child.

My healing began when I stopped performing and started simply showing up. And even when I knock with trembling hands, He opens the door with kindness.

Call to Action

Have you stopped asking because you've stopped believing He'll answer?

Try again.

Ask boldly. Seek relentlessly. Knock gently or with force—**but don't stop**. This is your part. Healing begins when you trust that your Father wants to open the door.

Prayer

Jesus,

I've been afraid to ask. Afraid You won't answer… or that I'm asking wrong. But You said to come. So here I am—asking, seeking, knocking. Help me trust in Your goodness and rest in Your timing. I know You are a Father who gives good gifts.

Amen.

THE GOLDEN RULE AND A HEALING LIFE

"So in everything, do to others what you would have them do to you, for this sums up the Law and the Prophets."
—Matthew 7:12

Contextual Reflection

This single sentence holds the heart of kingdom living. The Golden Rule is not just a call to be nice; it's the outworking of love. It requires humility, patience, and a willingness to see others through God's eyes. When we're tired, triggered, or wounded, this command exposes how fragile our self-control can be. Yet this is the fruit of healing: as God restores our relationship with Him, He restores how we see ourselves and how we respond to others.

Living by this rule reflects the Kingdom breaking into daily life. It shifts our focus from self-preservation to self-giving love. Jesus isn't giving us a suggestion; He's giving us the blueprint for relationships that mirror heaven.[2,4,6]

Personal Application

When I first stepped into healing, I thought it was just about fixing what was broken inside me. But Jesus showed me it also had to reshape how I treated others. For much of my life, my pattern wasn't to lash out, it was to withdraw. When people hurt me, I bit my tongue and moved on. I thought I was protecting others from pain, but really, I was protecting myself from rejection. I abandoned others before they could abandon me, and as a result, I didn't have many long-term relationships.

But I don't live that way anymore. In my healing, I've learned how to talk to people and share my feelings instead of hiding them. I've learned to stay present, to nurture relationships, and to practice honesty even when it feels vulnerable. I'm still very much a work in progress, but this scripture reminds me: if I want to be loved, I must first love.

The Golden Rule calls me to meet people where they are, just as I long for them to meet me where I am. It's no longer about cutting off or protecting myself, it's about building trust, choosing presence, and practicing the kind of love I hope to receive.

Call to Action

Take an honest look at your patterns in relationships and ask:

- *Do I tend to withdraw when hurt, lash out in anger, or try to protect myself by shutting down? Or do I lean in, stay present, and practice the love I long to receive?*
- *God, will You show me one relationship where I can live this rule more intentionally?*

Choose one small step, such as sharing how you feel, staying present in a hard moment, or offering kindness where you once would have pulled away.

Prayer

Jesus,

You distilled the law and the prophets into one golden thread—love others as I long to be loved. Teach me to live this not in theory, but in practice. Heal the parts of me that still react out of fear or pain. Help me slow down, stay present, and reflect Your heart in my daily choices.

Amen.

WALKING THE NARROW ROAD

"Enter through the narrow gate. For wide is the gate and broad is the road that leads to destruction, and many enter through it. But small is the gate and narrow the road that leads to life, and only a few find it." —Matthew 7:13-14

Contextual Reflection

Jesus paints a picture of two paths: one wide and easy, the other narrow and difficult. The broad road is crowded. It's the way of self-reliance, pride, and chasing after what feels good in the moment. It doesn't take effort to drift onto it; in fact, it feels natural.

The narrow road, by contrast, doesn't just symbolize morality—it is surrender, obedience, and alignment with God's will. It's less traveled because it costs something. It asks us to lay down our illusions of control and admit we can't save ourselves. It demands honesty, humility, and trust.

This isn't about earning our way into heaven but about walking daily in relationship with the One who leads us there. The narrow road is less about perfection and more about persistence—choosing to follow Jesus even when the way is steep and lonely. [2,4,6]

Personal Application

For years, I was on the broad road without realizing it. I thought I was just surviving, doing what I needed to get by. Really, I was drifting without direction, numbing my pain, and leaning on my own strength. I didn't see it as a "path," but looking back, it was a road that led me further from peace and closer to destruction.

Walking the narrow road now means choosing differently every day. It means pausing to ask: *Does this choice align with God's will, or with my old survival patterns?* Sometimes that looks like setting boundaries, sometimes it looks like staying present when I want to run, and sometimes it looks like trusting God when I can't see the outcome.

It isn't easy. There are days I stumble, days I want to take shortcuts, days I long for the wide road's false comfort. But here's the difference: I know Who is walking with me now. And even when the path feels hidden or hard, I trust that Jesus is leading me to life.

Call to Action

Take some time to reflect:

- *Am I truly walking the narrow road, or just admiring it from a distance?*
- *What old patterns or comforts tempt me back toward the broad road?*

Prayer

God,

Thank You for the invitation to the narrow road. I know it's not easy, but I don't want easy anymore—I want You. Lead me with courage when the way feels steep. Strengthen me when I stumble. And remind me that even the hardest road is worth it when I walk it with You.

Amen.

"Watch out for false prophets. They come to you in sheep's clothing, but inwardly they are ferocious wolves... Thus, by their fruit you will recognize them." —Matthew 7:15-20

Contextual Reflection

Jesus warns us to look past appearances. A person can sound spiritual or hold authority, but fruit tells the truth. Good fruit reflects God's Spirit—love, peace, kindness. Bad fruit leaves fear, harm, or control. The test isn't charisma or credentials, it's what their life produces.

And His words aren't only about others. They invite me to ask: what's growing in me? My fruit reveals where I'm rooted. [2,4,6]

Personal Application

I've seen firsthand the devastation of bad fruit through false prophets and spiritual manipulation that twisted God's Word for control. Those experiences left scars and created deep mistrust in me. For a long time, it made me question every voice that claimed authority.

But I've also had to face the bad fruit that took root in my own heart. Lies from abuse shaped the way I saw myself: worthless, unwanted, unlovable. Those seeds weren't planted by God, yet they grew until I let Him begin uprooting them. Healing for me has been a process of letting Jesus cut down what was rotten and plant something new in its place.

Now, when I inspect the fruit of my life, I see both the areas still in progress and the places where His Spirit is clearly at work. I see patience where there used to be avoidance. I see courage where fear used to rule. I see love beginning to flow where shame once silenced me. That's not me—it's Him, growing good fruit in a tree that once felt barren.

Call to Action

Pause and inspect the fruit:

- *What kind of fruit is growing in me? Does it reflect God's Spirit or my old wounds?*
- *Where do I need to invite Jesus to prune so healthier fruit can grow?*

Prayer

Jesus,

Help me see the truth. Give me eyes to recognize good fruit and the courage to walk away from what is rotten. Uproot the lies and heal what's still growing wild in me. Make me a tree rooted in You, bearing fruit that gives life.

Amen.

> *Not everyone who says to me, 'Lord, Lord,' will enter the kingdom of heaven, but only the one who does the will of my Father who is in heaven.*
>
> *Many will say to me on that day, 'Lord, Lord, did we not prophesy in your name and in your name drive out demons and in your name perform many miracles?'*
>
> *Then I will tell them plainly, 'I never knew you. Away from me, you evildoers!' —Matthew 7:21-23*

Contextual Reflection

This is one of the most sobering warnings in Jesus' entire sermon. These people aren't outsiders, they're active participants in ministry! They know His name. They do impressive works. But Jesus says He never knew them. This is a wake-up call to anyone who confuses activity for intimacy.

Jesus isn't impressed by spiritual resumes. He's after relationship. Doing God's will flows out of knowing God. This passage reminds us that faith isn't a performance; it's a posture of surrender, obedience, and love.[2,4,6]

Personal Application

I used to live in "fake it till you make it" Christianity. I knew I didn't really know Jesus. I didn't pray regularly. I didn't read the Word. I just went to church and served because I thought that was the formula. Deep down, I hoped I could just skate by on someone else's coattails.

But when I fell in love with Jesus, everything changed. I went from "I have no idea what being a Christian really means" to "I'm all in, God." Within just a couple months, He had flipped my whole life around. And here's the miracle: He never left me. He never gave up on me. He already knew who I was becoming.

Now, I don't serve to earn anything. I serve because I know Him. Because I love Him. Because I want to stay in His will. That's the foundation that can't be faked.

Call to Action

Take a moment to ask:

- *Am I doing things for Jesus without really knowing Him?*

He isn't looking for your checklist, He wants your heart. Take time to ask Him where your faith has been based on works, and where He wants to draw you closer. Your healing starts in intimacy, not performance.

Prayer

Jesus,

I don't want to just wear Your name, I want to know You. Pull me close. Show me where I've substituted effort for connection. Thank You for never giving up on me, even when I didn't know You. I want to walk in Your will, fully known and fully loved.

Amen.

> *"Therefore everyone who hears these words of mine and puts them into practice is like a wise man who built his house on the rock. The rain came down, the streams rose, and the winds blew and beat against that house; yet it did not fall, because it had its foundation on the rock. But everyone who hears these words of mine and does not put them into practice is like a foolish man who built his house on sand.*
>
> *The rain came down, the streams rose, and the winds blew and beat against that house, and it fell with a great crash."*
> *—Matthew 7:24-27*

Contextual Reflection

This closing passage of the Sermon on the Mount is a powerful call to action. Jesus makes it clear: it's not enough to hear His words; we must live them. The storm hits both houses. Faith doesn't protect us from hardship, but it does determine whether we stand or fall.

The rock foundation is not just belief in Jesus, it's trust and obedience. It's putting His words into practice daily. In contrast, sand may look smooth and comfortable, but it shifts. Building on it might feel easier at first, but it cannot hold when life gets rough. Jesus isn't shaming us, He's showing us how to live secure, even in the storm. [2,4,6]

Personal Application

I spent most of my life building my identity on sand. I didn't believe I was worthy. I didn't know much about myself because I'd been in survival mode for so long. So, I clung to the words of other people, letting their opinions define me.

If someone praised me, I felt valuable. If someone criticized me, I crumbled. I had no real foundation, just the shifting sands of human approval. I was stuck in performance, trying to 'be enough' for everyone else, not realizing that Jesus had already declared me enough in Him.

Everything changed when I fell in love with Jesus. I finally surrendered. I let Him speak into my identity. And through His red letters, I've begun to rebuild on solid rock. I no longer define myself by the labels other people gave me. I let His words tell me who I am.

Now, when the storms hit, as they always will, I don't fall apart like I used to. I may sway, I may cry, but I don't collapse. Because my life is finally being built on the truth of who He is and who He says I am.

Call to Action

Take a moment to ask:

- *What is my foundation built on?*

If it's anything but Jesus, the cracks will eventually show. But the good news is, rebuilding can start today. His words are strong enough to hold you. Let Him define your worth, steady your steps, and carry you through the storm.

Prayer

Jesus,

I've built on sand for too long. I'm tired of crashing every time life gets hard. Teach me how to build on You. Show me how to trust Your words more than the voices of others. You are my foundation now. Make me strong in You.

Amen.

I AM WILLING

"I am willing," he said. "Be clean! ...See that you don't tell anyone. But go, show yourself to the priest and offer the gift Moses commanded, as a testimony to them" —Matthew 8:3-4

Contextual Reflection

When a man with leprosy knelt before Jesus and said, *"Lord, if you are willing, you can make me clean,"* Jesus didn't hesitate. He reached out and touched him.

Leprosy in the first century was a life sentence of exclusion. People with leprosy were cut off from family, community, and worship, declared untouchable and erased from society. Yet this man boldly broke through every cultural barrier of fear and shame to reach Jesus. Instead of recoiling, Jesus reached out, touched him, and declared healing. In that one moment, He didn't just restore the man's body, He restored his humanity.

Jesus' touch showed that compassion comes before cure. And then He instructed the man to show himself to the priest and offer the gift Moses commanded. This wasn't about secrecy for secrecy's sake, it was about testimony. The healing wasn't just personal; it was meant to be seen, confirmed, and declared as evidence of God's power. [2,3,4]

Personal Application

Shame can be as isolating as leprosy. I carried wounds that screamed loudly: *"You're too broken. Too much. Unworthy."* For years, I wore the label Christian, but I wasn't really following Christ. I knew the language, I sang the songs, I nodded at the sermons, and even served, but deep down I kept the real me locked away. I wasn't willing to let Him into the places I thought were too messy, too painful, too unfixable.

That changed when I finally surrendered. I let Him into the parts of me I had hidden for decades. I confessed the bitterness, the habits I clung to, the ways I cut myself off from people before they could leave me. And instead of recoiling, He met me with love.

Surrender became the doorway to freedom. Suddenly, decisions that once felt impossible—like setting boundaries, speaking truth, or risking vulnerability—became acts of faith. I stopped living for appearances and started living from trust. Like the leper, I kneel before Him now not with fear, but with faith that dares to ask: *"If You are willing..."* and hearing Him answer, *"I am willing."*

Call to Action

I will bring my hidden places to Jesus:

- *Confess what I've been afraid to name out loud.*
- *Lay my shame and struggles at His feet in prayer.*
- *Trust that His willingness is greater than my self-doubt.*
- *Choose to believe that His touch can restore what shame told me was lost.*

Prayer

Jesus,

Thank You for touching the places in me I thought were untouchable. Heal not only my body, but also my heart, my identity, and my belonging. Help me live as a testimony of Your power and love. I receive Your willingness today.

Amen.

JUST SAY THE WORD

"Shall I come heal him?" —Matthew 8:7

"Truly I tell you, I have not found anyone in Israel with such great faith. I say to you that many will come from the east and the west and will take their places at the feast with Abraham, Isaac and Jacob in the kingdom of heaven. But the subjects of the kingdom will be thrown outside, into the darkness, where there will be weeping and gnashing of teeth. Go! Let it be done just as you believed it would."
—Matthew 8:10-13

Contextual Reflection

A Roman centurion, an outsider in every religious sense, came to Jesus on behalf of his paralyzed servant. The centurion wasn't Jewish, yet he understood Jesus' authority more than those who claimed to know God. He knew power when he saw it. He didn't need a sign. He didn't need Jesus to be physically present. He trusted that one word carried enough authority to change everything. [2,3,4,6]

Personal Application

I've often tied my healing to performance toward Him:

If I serve on enough committees, I will earn enough grace.

When I accomplish what others have, I'll be worthy.

When I start reading my Bible daily, then He will love me.

But faith that heals trusts Jesus even when He feels far away. Healing doesn't wait for proximity—it responds to His authority.

This moment with the centurion shows that Jesus did not come for one group of people, but for ALL people. It reminds me that I don't have to be perfect to fall into His grace. He loves me just the way I am, just where I am—wounds, scabs, and scars included—and if I let Him, He will heal them all.

Like the centurion, I'm learning to pray: *"Lord, just say the word."* Healing may or may not come instantly, but His authority speaks into my anxiety, my wounds, my doubts. Every time I choose to trust His word over my fear, I experience a piece of that healing freedom.

Call to Action

Take a moment to ask:

- *Where in my life do I need to hear Jesus speak the word?*

Name that place honestly. Then choose one step you can take today that shows you believe His authority is already at work.

Prayer

Lord,

Give me faith like the centurion. Let me believe in Your word more than I believe in my circumstances. Speak, and let my soul be healed.

Amen.

COUNT THE COST

"Foxes have dens and birds have nests, but the Son of Man has no place to lay his head." —Matthew 8:20

"Follow me, and let the dead bury their own dead." —Matthew 8:22

Contextual Reflection

A teacher of the law said, *"I will follow you wherever you go."*

A disciple asked to delay following Jesus until after his father's funeral.

In this passage, Jesus makes it clear: following Him won't be easy or convenient. It will mean choosing Him above comfort, security, and even cultural expectations. He doesn't promise stability—He promises Himself. When He said, "Let the dead bury their own dead," He wasn't being callous about grief. He was pointing to the urgency of spiritual life—that we can't stay stuck in the ways of the world while delaying obedience. True life is found in Him and following Him brings us out of spiritual deadness into freedom. [2,4,6]

Personal Application

For a long time, I thought following Christ meant I had to instantly give up every sin and strip away all worldly things. When I couldn't, I felt ashamed and unworthy, convinced that I lacked the self-control required to be a true disciple. But I've learned that God doesn't judge me for not changing everything at once. He meets me where I am and patiently helps me face each struggle one at a time. Jesus doesn't reject me for my imperfections. He embraces them, loving me through the process until He and I work them out together.

Following Him into healing has meant releasing things I once thought I needed—relationships, habits, and false identities that only gave the illusion of safety. Letting go hasn't been easy. Sometimes healing requires saying goodbye to what numbed me or stepping into uncomfortable vulnerability. Yet each time I choose Him instead of delay, He fills the empty spaces with something greater—peace, joy, and a deeper sense of belonging.

Call to Action

Take a moment to ask:

- *What's one thing I've been holding onto that blocks my healing?*

Name it honestly. Then decide: will I keep carrying it, or will I place it in Jesus' hands and let Him fill that space with something greater?

Prayer

Jesus,

Help me follow You without delay or excuse. Even when healing feels costly, remind me that You are worth more than anything I leave behind.

Amen.

PEACE IN THE STORM

"You of little faith, why are you so afraid?"
—Matthew 8:26

Contextual Reflection

Jesus was asleep in the boat when a violent storm broke out. The disciples panicked and cried out, *"Lord, save us!"* He got up, rebuked the wind and the waves—and there was great calm.

For seasoned fishermen, this storm wasn't minor. Their fear was real. But Jesus, unshaken, revealed that His presence carries more weight than any storm. When He called them people of "little faith," He wasn't dismissing them but reminding them that even small trust could grow when rooted in Him. Their problem wasn't no faith; it was underdeveloped faith. He doesn't just command nature; He embodies peace and calls us to trust Him more deeply. [1,2,4,6]

Personal Application

In my own storms—panic attacks, trauma triggers, nights of fear—I've begged Jesus to wake up. Sometimes He calms the chaos at once. Other times, His first gift is showing me what peace looks like while the storm still rages.

This helps me see that my faith is still quite young. It isn't fully formed yet, but like the disciples, I'm learning to lean more deeply into Jesus so that faith can grow stronger. I must feed that seed—watering it with trust, prayer, and obedience. That's why God led me into this red-letter study: so, I can experience Jesus for myself and hear what He says about me. I've depended on the world for my identity for too long. Now it's time to learn the truth through Jesus' words.

Healing has meant discovering that His presence in my boat is enough. I don't have to control the waves or outrun the storm. I can rest knowing He's with me.

Peace isn't the absence of chaos; it's the presence of Jesus.

Call to Action

When anxiety, panic, or fear rises, pause and breathe deeply. Say out loud, *"Jesus is in my boat."* Repeat this as many times as you need. Practice resting in His peace instead of rehearsing your fear.

Prayer

Lord,

When fear rises like a storm inside me, remind me You are here. Still my soul with Your peace until the waves obey Your word.

Amen.

THE AUTHORITY OF ONE WORD

"Go!" —Matthew 8:32

Contextual Reflection

Two men possessed by demons confronted Jesus, and with one command—simply "Go!"—He sent the evil spirits out of them and into a herd of pigs that immediately plunged into the water. One word. That's all it took.

The same Jesus who calms storms with a rebuke casts out darkness with a single syllable. His authority is not contested—it is absolute. Darkness knows His voice and flees.[2,4,6]

Personal Application

I've carried inner tormentors: voices of shame, memories that chained me, lies that told me I was unworthy. For years, they dictated my thoughts, convincing me that peace was for everyone else but me. I learned how to hide behind smiles, but inside, those old echoes screamed louder than truth.

Now, in this stage of my faith, I'm learning that when the enemy stirs those feelings, I don't have to listen. I can call on the one-word power of Jesus and say with authority, "Go!" In His name, the tormentors lose their grip. Sometimes that command is spoken in strength, and other times it's whispered through tears, but it still carries the same power.

Healing begins with His authority spoken in faith. It's not about shouting louder; it's about standing firmer in the truth that darkness no longer owns me. Each time fear or shame rises, I practice saying what He says: "Go!" This isn't denial; it's defiance against the lies that once controlled me.

Every time I do, I feel that weight lift a little more. The same Jesus who drove out the demons now drives out my doubts, my self-hatred, my guilt. This is how I grow my faith: by living in His Word, accepting the grace that baptizes me in His power, and choosing to remain in it instead of only testing the water with my toes.

Call to Action

When lies or fears surface, don't argue with them, command them to leave in Jesus' name. Speak out loud, *"Go!"* and invite His truth to take their place.

Prayer

Jesus,

I receive Your authority in my life. Speak to the places still chained in fear and darkness and drive them out. Teach me to echo Your word with courage: *Go!*

Amen.

> *"Take heart, son; your sins are forgiven."*
> *—Matthew 9:2*
>
> *"Why do you entertain evil thoughts in your hearts? Which is easier: to say, 'Your sins are forgiven,' or to say, 'Get up and walk'? But I want you to know that the Son of Man has authority on earth to forgive sins" ... "Get up, take your mat and go home." —Matthew 9:4-6*

Contextual Reflection

Some men brought to Jesus a paralyzed man lying on a mat. Seeing their faith, Jesus told the man that his sins were forgiven. The teachers of the law were outraged, whispering accusations of blasphemy—how could any man claim the power to forgive sin? But Jesus, knowing their thoughts, responded with both compassion and authority.

In that moment, He tied forgiveness and healing together, revealing that our deepest need isn't physical but spiritual. His words directly confronted the religious leaders who believed only God could forgive sins, because Jesus was openly claiming divine authority. Yet by healing the man's body with a word, He gave visible proof of an invisible reality: He carried the authority not only to restore broken bodies but also to forgive sin and heal the soul at its root. [2,3,4,6]

Personal Application

As a child, I saw this story only through the awe of physical healing. I thought if Jesus could make a paralyzed man walk, He could change my mom and end the suffering in our home. I prayed so hard for her to "get up and walk" out of those circumstances, but it never happened. I still clung to Jesus for a time, but by sixteen, anger and disappointment had me convinced this scripture was a farce. I felt betrayed that the miracle never came.

Years later, at forty-eight, I entered Celebrate Recovery. That's when my perspective shifted, and I realized Jesus had been sending people all along to help me "get up and walk" toward Him. I was carrying my mat out of my mom's house and into His house. Hindsight showed me that as a child I had leaned on Him, and He truly did save me, even if I couldn't see it then. His forgiveness and presence were there before restoration, and now I see that was the foundation of my lasting healing.

Call to Action

Take a moment to ask:

- *Am I only seeking Jesus for healing in my body or circumstances, or am I also inviting Him to forgive and free my soul?*
- *What would it look like to truly let His words, "Take heart," shape my identity today?*

Prayer

Jesus,

Thank You for forgiving me and lifting the weight of shame. Heal my heart as You heal my body and circumstances. I take heart in Your authority.

Amen.

> *"Follow me." —Matthew 9:9*
>
> *"It is not the healthy who need a doctor, but the sick. But go and learn what this means: 'I desire mercy, not sacrifice.' For I have not come to call the righteous, but sinners."*
> *—Matthew 9:12-13*

Contextual Reflection

As Jesus went on, He saw Matthew the tax collector sitting at his booth and simply said, "Follow me." Later, when Jesus dined with Matthew, surrounded by other tax collectors and sinners, the Pharisees questioned Him for keeping such company. Jesus responded that He came not for the righteous, but for those in need of mercy.

Matthew was an outsider, despised as a traitor to his people. Tax collectors were often viewed as corrupt, profiting from Rome's oppression and their own people's pain. Yet Jesus' call carried both risk and honor: it meant leaving behind wealth, reputation, and shame to step into discipleship. By sharing a meal with those labeled "unworthy," Jesus revealed His mission—to seek the sick and sinful, not the self-righteous. He redefined holiness as mercy, not rigid rule-keeping, showing that God's Kingdom was open to everyone society had written off. [2,3,4,6]

Personal Application

Like Matthew, I've felt the sting of rejection and unworthiness. Growing up poor, I carried rejection everywhere—at home, at school, and even in church. Though some of God's people reached out, took me to church, and loved me as Jesus taught, I was often labeled the charity case. I felt looked down upon for my mother's choices, and that judgment cut deeply. It wasn't fair, it wasn't right, and it certainly wasn't from God.

Yet even then, I sensed the difference. I gravitated toward those who welcomed me as a child of God regardless of my circumstances. In them, I caught glimpses of Jesus, they embodied His mercy. At the same time, the constant criticism pushed me into striving for perfection. I believed that to be worthy of God's love, I had to be flawless because I perceived God's people as flawless, and to fit in, I had to measure up.

Only later, as I returned to this scripture, did I finally understand: Jesus never asked for perfection before extending His call. He simply said, "Follow me." Healing began when I stopped chasing the approval of the judgmental and instead rested fully in His mercy and love, trusting His judgment of my heart rather than my outward appearance or financial status.

Call to Action

Take a moment to ask:

- *What excuses have I been holding onto that keep me from fully walking with Jesus?*
- *How can I respond to His invitation today with honesty and surrender?*
- *Where is He calling me to practice mercy—especially toward those who are unwanted or overlooked?*

Prayer

Jesus,

Thank You for calling me as I am. Teach me to follow You with mercy, not performance. Let me offer others the same compassion You give me.

Amen.

NEW WINE

"How can the guests of the bridegroom mourn while he is with them? The time will come when the bridegroom will be taken from them; then they will fast. No one sews a patch of unshrunk cloth on an old garment... Neither do people pour new wine into old wineskins. If they do, the skins will burst... No, they pour new wine into new wineskins, and both are preserved." —Matthew 9:15-17

Contextual Reflection

When asked why His disciples didn't fast like others, Jesus answered by using two simple yet profound images—a wedding and wineskins. Both carried deep meaning for His listeners.

A wedding was a time of joy and new beginnings; the presence of the bridegroom symbolized celebration, not mourning. In other words, fasting would be out of place while the Bridegroom, Jesus Himself, was present with them.

Wineskins, on the other hand, illustrated the need for flexibility. New wine expands and would burst old, rigid skins. In the same way, His presence brought something entirely new that couldn't be contained by the old religious systems or traditions. Jesus wasn't offering a patch or a temporary fix; He was bringing transformation. [2,3,4,6]

Personal Application

I can't pour His new life into my old ways of coping and expect it to work. Healing requires new space, including habits, perspectives, and surrender. For some, transformation happens in an instant; for others, it unfolds slowly over years. I have a friend who was healed from alcoholism in one night—the very night she became a believer in Christ. For me, full surrender took fourteen years. Letting go can be harder for some of us, which makes the healing journey longer. There is no set timeframe to transform, just lean into Christ and take one thing at a time, one day at a time, and one moment at a time. If I cling to my old "wineskins," I risk missing the fullness of His Spirit. But when I allow Him to make me new, His healing expands within me.

Call to Action

Take a moment to ask:

- *What "old wineskin" am I still holding onto; an unhealthy pattern, coping mechanism, or rigid belief that no longer serves where God is leading me?*
- *How is Jesus inviting me to release it and make room for something new?*

Invite Jesus to replace them with something new that can hold His transforming power.

Prayer

Lord,

Make me a new wineskin. Stretch my faith and prepare me for Your Spirit's new wine. Help me release what no longer serves Your purpose, so I can be fully ready for the new thing You are doing. Preserve me by Your presence.

Amen.

"Take courage, daughter; your faith has healed you."
—Matthew 9:22

"Go away. The girl is not dead but asleep." —Matthew 9:24

Contextual Reflection

A synagogue leader pleaded for his daughter's life. On His way to the home, a woman who had been bleeding for twelve years reached out and touched the edge of Jesus' cloak, believing even a touch could heal her. Jesus turned and said, "Take courage, daughter; your faith has healed you."

When He arrived at the leader's house and saw mourners weeping, He said, "Go away. The girl is not dead but asleep." The crowd laughed in disbelief—yet Jesus took her by the hand, and she got up.

In both encounters, Jesus stopped for those who had been overlooked. To the outcast woman, He gave dignity by calling her "daughter." In a culture that had shunned her for twelve years, that word restored her identity as beloved. To the grieving father, He gave hope beyond human limits. Jesus brought life where there was death and hope where there was despair, not only healing bodies but also reclaiming worth in the eyes of others. Faith drew Him near, and His authority raised what others declared lost, proving that no amount of human rejection can stand against His compassion and power. [1,2,3,4,6]

Personal Application

I know what it feels like to silently suffer, hoping no one notices my pain. I've been the outcast in so many places in this world, but Jesus welcomed me with open arms. He doesn't abandon us; we are the ones who so often abandon Him. For twenty years, I turned away from Him, angry and closed off, yet He never stopped placing steppingstones in my path. Even in my rebellion, He was shaping my future, building skills, and molding me for what was to come. Jesus doesn't leave us in our pain; it is usually we who choose to isolate ourselves, thinking it's safer to shut off the real aches of the soul out of fear, guilt, anger, or hurt. Yet even then, He whispers hope. He calls me daughter, restores dignity before the crowd, and where I thought hope was dead, He shows me it is only asleep. Healing begins when we stop hiding and allow Him to mend our souls. It is both intimate and powerful—He meets me in secret and raises me in public.

Call to Action

Take a moment to ask:

- *What part of me do I need to surrender to Jesus?*

Reach out to Him in faith, even if only with trembling hands. Believe that He sees you, calls you His own, and restores what feels dead.

Prayer

Jesus,

Thank You for seeing me when I feel invisible. Heal my hidden wounds and awaken hope where I thought it was gone.

Amen.

Do You Believe?

"Do you believe that I am able to do this?" —Matthew 9:28

"According to your faith let it be done to you. See that no one knows about this." —Matthew 9:29-30

Contextual Reflection

Two blind men followed Jesus, crying out for mercy. When He asked if they believed He could heal them, they answered, "Yes, Lord." With a touch, their eyes were opened, and their sight was restored. Soon after, Jesus also freed a man possessed by a demon, again displaying His complete authority over both physical and spiritual bondage.

Faith and healing are inseparable in this passage. Jesus didn't ask to test their belief but to draw it forward—to reveal that faith is the channel through which His power flows. Their "yes" opened the door for sight and freedom, showing that trust in Him is not passive but active. It requires both a heart response and a step of courage, and when they offered both, His power moved. This reminds us that faith is less about quantity and more about willingness—to place what little we have into His hands and trust that He will make it enough. [2,3,4,6]

Personal Application

In the past, my prayers often wavered in belief, half-hoping God would come through. But here, Jesus asks me directly: "Do you believe I am able?" For much of my life I lived this very reality, always hiding my true self, ashamed of my past, fearful of rejection, avoiding judgment, and carrying guilt. I grew up believing these things defined me, only seeing my identity as an abused child. I hid it as best I could, even getting better at hiding over time. Yet Jesus showed me that hiding is only avoidance, and it only hurts me. My healing requires more than hope—it requires trust in His power and a willingness to come out of hiding. It wasn't comfortable nor was it easy, but coming out of hiding was the best thing I ever did, it was freedom wrapped in honesty. Each time I say, "Yes, Lord," I open my life to His restoring touch and allow Him to redefine me beyond my past.

Call to Action

Take a moment to ask:

- *When Jesus asks, "Do you believe I am able?"—how do I respond?*
- *Am I praying with confident faith, or am I still hiding parts of myself out of fear or doubt?*
- *What step of courage can I take today to say, "Yes, Lord," and open my life to His restoring touch?*

Prayer

Lord,

I believe. Strengthen my faith where it wavers. Touch my life with Your healing hand and restore my sight—both physical and spiritual.

Amen.

THE TWELVE ARE SENT OUT

"Do not go among the Gentiles or enter any town of the Samaritans. Go rather to the lost sheep of Israel. As you go, proclaim this message: 'The kingdom of heaven has come near.' Heal the sick, raise the dead, cleanse those who have leprosy, drive out demons. Freely you have received; freely give." —Matthew 10:5-8

Contextual Reflection

Jesus called His twelve disciples and gave them authority to drive out impure spirits and heal every disease. The mission began with the twelve, but it was not about power or prestige—it was about service. Jesus entrusted them with His authority, not to make them important, but to make them useful. Their work was rooted in compassion: healing, restoring, proclaiming the nearness of God. His command to "freely give" reminded them that what they carried was never theirs to own; it was a gift meant to be shared. [2,4,6]

Personal Application

There was a time when I wanted to keep my healing tucked safely inside, like a fragile treasure between me and God. After everything I'd been through, it felt sacred—too personal, too tender to share. But Jesus keeps reminding me that healing isn't meant to be hoarded; it's meant to be multiplied.

In this passage, He sent the disciples out to heal, restore, and proclaim the nearness of God. That same command still stands today. Healing is not complete when I'm merely made whole, it deepens when I help others find wholeness too. Sharing my story doesn't make my wounds reopen; it lets others see that scars can become symbols of grace.

Learning to accept others as they are has been part of that healing. I don't have to fix them, convince them, or rush their process. I'm learning to meet people where they are, just as Jesus met me. Sometimes the most healing thing I can do is listen, love, and let my story remind them they're not alone.

My healing journey has become a mission of giving away what was freely given to me. When I speak about what God has done in my life, I'm not showing off—I'm simply passing along the gift of hope. Healing isn't just something I received; it's something I now get to share.

Call to Action

Name one false security you've been holding on to. Take it to God through prayer and take one step of faith to trust Him with just this one thing. When you are ready, add another.

Prayer

Jesus,

I lay my false sense of security at your feet and ask that You strip away the things I cling to. Teach me to trust Your provision and rest in the peace You give.

Amen.

> *"Do not get any gold or silver or copper to take with you in your belts—no bag for the journey or extra shirt or sandals or a staff, for the worker is worth his keep. Whatever town or village you enter, search there for some worthy person and stay at their house until you leave. As you enter the home, give it your greeting. If the home is deserving, let your peace rest on it; if it is not, let your peace return to you. If anyone will not welcome you or listen to your words, leave that home or town and shake the dust off your feet. Truly I tell you, it will be more bearable for Sodom and Gomorrah on the day of judgment than for that town." —Matthew 10:9-15*

Contextual Reflection

Jesus stripped away their safety nets. They were not to depend on money, possessions, or plans, but on God's provision through others. This wasn't reckless, it was trust. Their peace was powerful; it could rest or return, depending on the reception. In sending them vulnerable, He made space for hospitality, generosity, and reliance on God's care through community.[2,4,6]

Personal Application

This passage feels like a mirror to my own journey of stepping into leadership within Celebrate Recovery. Jesus told His disciples to travel light—no money, no extra clothes, no backup plan—because their provision would come from God through the people they served. That's what Principle 8 and Step 12 have taught me: to trust Him enough to give away what was freely given to me.

When I began serving in leadership, I realized that healing deepens when we pour it back out. I don't have to carry everything with me or have all the answers. I just have to show up, willing and available, and let God do the rest. That's the heart of recovery: receiving grace, then becoming a vessel for it.

There was a time when I thought my healing was just for me—a quiet victory between God and me. But Jesus keeps showing me it's meant to be shared. Each time I speak, lead, or listen, I'm reminded that my story was never wasted—it's a tool for someone else's breakthrough. *LUMARISE* is an extension of that same calling: a place to share my journey so that others might find healing, too.

Living out Principle 8 and Step 12 keeps me grounded. They remind me that recovery isn't the end of the story—it's the beginning of service. I'm not healed to sit still; I'm healed to carry peace wherever I go and trust that God will provide what I need for the journey.

Call to Action

Think about one area where you're relying on your own safety net and take a moment to ask:

- *How might I step out in trust this week and allow God to provide through others?*

Prayer

Lord,

Help me release my need for control and trust You to provide in unexpected ways. Teach me to rest in Your peace and depend on Your care through community.

Amen.

SHEEP AMONG WOLVES

"I am sending you out like sheep among wolves. Therefore be as shrewd as snakes and as innocent as doves. Be on your guard; you will be handed over to the local councils and be flogged in the synagogues. But when they arrest you, do not worry about what to say or how to say it. At that time you will be given what to say, for it will not be you speaking, but the Spirit of your Father speaking through you."
—Matthew 10:16-20

Contextual Reflection

Jesus did not sugarcoat the mission. He warned of danger, opposition, and rejection. Yet His promise was not escape, it was presence. The Spirit would give words in the moment. The imagery of sheep among wolves captured both vulnerability and dependence. His disciples were not to be naïve but to walk in both wisdom and purity, grounded in trust that God Himself would speak through them. [2,4,6]

Personal Application

I've faced people and situations that tore me down, leaving me speechless. But Jesus promises that I don't have to fight with my own words; His Spirit will speak through me.

I've had this experience already: so many people make promises yet do not deliver. I am learning to step outside my comfort zone to ask for help, and I'm discovering that some respond, but most don't.

Jesus didn't say this would be easy; He made that clear in this very scripture. I've found it certainly is not, but the joy of doing the one thing I was put here to do is reward beyond measure.

God directs me, Jesus loves me, and the Holy Spirit gives me discernment. The perfect trifecta that places a barrier of protection around me. Healing has meant learning to pause and trust that I don't always need to defend myself. When I stay rooted in Him, I can respond with both strength and gentleness. Even in hostile spaces, His Spirit equips me with what I need.

Call to Action

The next time you feel attacked or misunderstood, pause before responding. Ask the Holy Spirit to give you words and trust Him to speak through you.

Prayer

Holy Spirit,

Fill me when I am afraid or unsure. Give me words that carry truth and love, even when I feel weak. Speak through me.

Amen.

PERSECUTION WARNING

"Brother will betray brother to death, and a father his child; children will rebel against their parents and have them put to death. You will be hated by everyone because of me, but the one who stands firm to the end will be saved. The student is not above the teacher, nor a servant above his master. If the head of the house has been called Beelzebul, how much more the members of his household!" —Matthew 10:21-25

Contextual Reflection

Following Jesus may result in division, even for the closest relationships. The cost of discipleship is real—betrayal, hatred, and slander. He reframes this suffering as part of sharing in His own life. If the Teacher endured rejection, His followers should not expect exemption. This is not only a reality of the ancient world but also of today; standing for Christ can strain families, friendships, workplaces, and even communities. Our culture often rewards compromise and silence, but Jesus calls us to endure with truth and love. The call is endurance, trusting that salvation belongs to those who stand firm, yesterday and today alike. [2,4,6]

Personal Application

People always let me down, and because I didn't trust others yet hated being alone, I wandered like a nomad—caught between craving acceptance and fearing abandonment. This restless search led to relationship addiction and repeated attempts to start over after damaging my reputation.

My relationships didn't fracture because of my faith—they fractured because I wrestled with abandonment, codependency, and a lack of faith. I spent many years inflicting pain on myself, torn between mistrust of others and fear of being alone. Then, God had me end my previous codependent relationship and just be with Him. I resisted for many months, but finally, I did as He asked.

In this scripture, Jesus reminds me that I'm not alone; He understands because He faced worse. Healing means anchoring my worth not in acceptance, not in others' opinions, and not in worldly things, but in belonging to Him. This anchor in Him is what finally freed me from the cycle of relationship addiction and codependence, breaking the very patterns that once kept me trapped.

Call to Action

Think of one relationship where following Jesus has cost you. Pray for that person and surrender your need for their approval, choosing instead to stand firm in Christ.

Prayer

Lord,

When rejection comes, remind me I am Yours. Give me endurance to stand firm and courage to follow You no matter the cost.

Amen.

Do Not Fear

> *"So do not be afraid of them, for there is nothing concealed that will not be disclosed, or hidden that will not be made known. What I tell you in the dark, speak in the daylight; what is whispered in your ear, proclaim from the roofs. Do not be afraid of those who kill the body but cannot kill the soul. Rather, be afraid of the One who can destroy both soul and body in hell... Even the very hairs of your head are all numbered. So don't be afraid; you are worth more than many sparrows. Whoever acknowledges me before others, I will also acknowledge before my Father in heaven. But whoever disowns me before others, I will disown before my Father in heaven."*
> *—Matthew 10:26-33*

Contextual Reflection

Jesus speaks straight to fear. Twice He says, "Do not be afraid." Fear loses its grip when we recognize both God's power and His intimate care. Our value to Him is unmatched—even the sparrows, small and common birds sold cheaply in the marketplace, are watched and cared for by God. If He pays attention to creatures the world considers insignificant, how much more does He value us? The mission may bring risk, but their security rests in God's sovereignty and His unwavering attention to even the smallest details of our lives. [2,4,6]

Personal Application

Fear has ruled much of my life—fear of rejection, failure, retaliation, and exposure. As a child, I highlighted every 'fear not' verse I could find in my Bible, marking them with pen, pencil, and highlighter alike. Living in constant fear at home, I clung to those red letters as my only refuge.

I remember at 14, refusing to go back to my mother's house because I feared for my life. Terrified, I threatened that if they forced me back, I would run away and turn to prostitution. That was the moment God gave me my first taste of 'fear not.' I was afraid, but He did not allow that fear to stop me from what had to be done. That day they placed me in a foster home.

Today, Jesus reminds me still that my worth is not fragile. God knows me so deeply that He counts even the hairs on my head. Healing for me has meant learning to live from this worth, not from fear. My soul is secure in Him, and no person or circumstance can take that away.

Call to Action

Take a moment to ask:

- *What fears still whisper that I'm not safe or worthy of love?*
- *How can I remind myself this week that my value is unshakable in God's eyes?*

When fear rises, pause and speak truth, "I am seen. I am known. I am worth more than sparrows."

Prayer

Father,

When fear threatens to overwhelm me, remind me of my worth in You. Help me proclaim truth boldly, knowing You hold my soul secure.

Amen

"Do not suppose that I have come to bring peace to the earth. I did not come to bring peace, but a sword. For I have come to turn 'a man against his father, a daughter against her mother...' Anyone who loves their father or mother more than me is not worthy of me; anyone who loves their son or daughter more than me is not worthy of me. Whoever does not take up their cross and follow me is not worthy of me. Whoever finds their life will lose it, and whoever loses their life for my sake will find it." —Matthew 10:34-39

Contextual Reflection

Jesus makes a radical claim: His presence divides. Allegiance to Him comes before even the strongest earthly ties. To "take up the cross" meant embracing shame and sacrifice—long before the cross became a symbol of victory, it was an instrument of death. True discipleship means dying to self, surrendering the life we try to build in order to find the life only He can give. [2,4,6]

Personal Application

I resisted surrender for years, terrified of losing the life I thought I needed. But Jesus showed me the cross is not just a decoration of victory—it was first an instrument of death and sacrifice. That is what He asked of me with *LUMARISE*: to lay down the career I had clung to for security and identity.

In this, I see His own path reflected—God sent Jesus to give everything for us. For me, it felt like a death to my 25–year career in instructional design, the very one He placed me in. I didn't choose it; He did. Yet He asked me to step away. This became my cross: leaving the familiar, stepping into the unknown world of nonprofit. And yes, it felt like loss. But in the letting go, I discovered something greater: joy, freedom, and the thrill of walking in His plan.

Healing has come not by holding tighter, but by opening my hands and letting Him reshape me. Obedience hasn't been easy, but its joy outweighs every loss. On the far side of surrender, I have found a life fuller and richer than anything I could have built on my own.

Call to Action

Take a moment to ask:

- *What is Jesus leading me toward right now?*
- *What areas might I begin loosening my grip on so you can walk closer with Him?*
- *How might I start working toward taking up my cross in this season?*

Invite Him to show you the next step and trust His timing as you follow.

Prayer

Jesus,

Teach me to love You above all else. Give me courage to surrender what I cannot keep, so I can receive the life only You can give.

Amen.

THE REWARD OF WELCOMING

"Anyone who welcomes you welcomes me, and anyone who welcomes me welcomes the one who sent me. Whoever welcomes a prophet as a prophet will receive a prophet's reward... And if anyone gives even a cup of cold water to one of these little ones who is my disciple, truly I tell you, that person will certainly not lose their reward."
—Matthew 10:40-42

Contextual Reflection

Jesus connects hospitality with Himself. To welcome His followers is to welcome Him, and ultimately the Father. No act of kindness is too small; God sees even a cup of cold water. He honors those who recognize His presence in others. The reward is not about status but about shared participation in God's mission. [2,3,4,6]

Personal Application

So much of my life, I felt unseen, unworthy, unwelcome, and unloved. As a child I wasn't well groomed, my clothes were tattered and stained, and I lived in roach-infested filth.

Jesus promises that when we welcome others, we are welcoming Him. Looking back, I see how God placed people in my childhood who lived this truth. No matter what, they welcomed me anyway. I can only imagine how hard it must have been for them to welcome this filthy child, but they did—living out the very words of Jesus in this passage. Their kindness planted seeds I still carry today.

Healing has been realizing that love is not built on grand gestures but on small, faithful acts of kindness. Even the smallest offering matters. Now, when I extend compassion, encouragement, and kindness, I feel as though I am carrying forward what was once given to me. God uses these small acts to build His kingdom.

Call to Action

Look for a simple way to welcome someone this week—whether through a kind word, an invitation, or a gesture of hospitality. Remember that in welcoming them, you are welcoming Him.

Prayer

Lord,

Help me welcome others as I would welcome You. Teach me to see Your presence in every person, and to trust that even the smallest act of love matters in Your kingdom.

Amen.

CLOSING REFLECTION

As you come to the end of this first volume, my hope is that you feel a little lighter, a little stronger, and a little more at peace. These pages have not been about perfection, but about process—the ongoing work of healing through love.

The words you've read are woven with pieces of my story. They carry my struggles, my questions, and my discoveries. But your journey is your own. What spoke to me may look different for you, and that's the beauty of it. Healing never follows one path. It bends, twists, and surprises us along the way.

If you've found encouragement, even a single spark of hope, then this book has done what it was meant to do. My prayer is that you carry that hope into your daily life, letting it grow in the quiet places where you need it most.

Remember this, you are not defined by the words spoken over you in anger or doubt. You are not the sum of your wounds. You are seen, worthy, welcome, and loved—right where you are, as you are.

This is only the beginning. Volume 2 will continue the journey, following the red-letter words further, opening up new spaces of reflection and healing. For now, take a deep breath. Celebrate how far you've come. And know that peace is not a destination you have to chase—it's something that begins to bloom inside you the moment you choose love.

RESOURCES

1. The Holy Bible, New International Version. Grand Rapids: Zondervan, 2011.

2. France, R.T. *The Gospel of Matthew. The New International Commentary on the New Testament.* Grand Rapids: Eerdmans, 2007.

3. Keener, Craig S. *The IVP Bible Background Commentary: New Testament.* Downers Grove: InterVarsity Press, 1993.

4. Nolland, John. *The Gospel of Matthew. The New International Greek Testament Commentary.* Grand Rapids: Eerdmans, 2005.

5. Wright, N.T. *Matthew for Everyone, Part 1.* Louisville: Westminster John Knox Press, 2004.

6. Green, Joel B., Scott McKnight, and I. Howard Marshall, eds. *Dictionary of Jesus and the Gospels.* Downers Grove: InterVarsity Press, 1992.

7. Ortberg, John. *If You Want to Walk on Water, You've Got to Get Out of the Boat.* Grand Rapids: Zondervan, 2001.

www.ingramcontent.com/pod-product-compliance
Lightning Source LLC
LaVergne TN
LVHW021122080426
835513LV00011B/1201